T0086802

Iowa's Forgotten General

Matthew Mark Trumbull, as Colonel of the 9th Iowa Cavalry
(*Courtesy State Historical Society of Iowa, Des Moines*)

Iowa's Forgotten General: Matthew Mark Trumbull and the Civil War

Kenneth L. Lyftogt

University of Iowa Press
Iowa City

University of Iowa Press, Iowa City 52242
www.uiowapress.org
Copyright © 2005 by Kenneth Lyftogt
All rights reserved
Originally published in 2005 by the Press of the Camp Pope Bookshop
www.camppope.com
Designed by Clark Kenyon
Printed in the United States of America
No part of this book may be reproduced or used in any form or by any means without permission in writing from the publisher. All reasonable steps have been taken to contact copyright holders of material used in this book. The publisher would be pleased to make suitable arrangements with any whom it has not been possible to reach.
The University of Iowa Press is a member of Green Press Initiative and is committed to preserving natural resources.

Printed on acid-free paper

Library of Congress Cataloging-in-Publication Data
Lyftogt, Kenneth.
Iowa's forgotten general: Matthew Mark Trumbull and the Civil War / by Kenneth L. Lyftogt.
          p.   cm.
Originally published: Iowa City, Iowa: Camp Pope Bookshop, 2005.
Includes bibliographical references and index.
ISBN-13: 978-1-58729-612-3 (paper)
ISBN-10: 1-58729-612-8 (paper)
        1. Trumbull, M. M. (Matthew Mark), 1826–1894.   2. Generals—United States—Biography.   3. United States. Army—Biography.   4. United States. Army. Iowa Infantry Regiment, 3rd (1861–1864).   5. United States. Army. Iowa Cavalry Regiment, 9th (1863–1866).   6. Iowa—History—Civil War, 1861–1865—Regimental histories.   7. Iowa—History—Civil War, 1861–1865—Biography.   8. United States—History—Civil War, 1861–1865—Regimental histories.   9. United States—History—Civil War, 1861–1865—Biography.   10. Iowa—Biography.   I. Title.
E467.1.T83L94 2007   2007008267
973.7'477092—dc22
[B]

07 08 09 10 11 P 5 4 3 2 1

To Hollis Miller with love and respect

Also by Kenneth L. Lyftogt:

Road Freaks of Trans-Amerika
Highway 13
From Blue Mills to Columbia: Cedar Falls and the Civil War
Left For Dixie: The Civil War Diary of John Rath

Table of Contents

Illustrations and Maps

Acknowledgements

This book would not have been written if not for the encouragement of three people: Mike Prahl, Ron Prahl, and John Higdon—friends and colleagues who listened to my stories of Matthew Trumbull. Ron Prahl edited the first two manuscript versions and also did the drawings included in the book. Chris Rossi, director of Humanities Iowa, used several stories from this book on "Voices of Humanities Iowa," a radio program on Iowa Pubic Radio. The State Historical Society of Iowa and the National Archives and Records Administration were extremely helpful in supplying necessary military records. A special thank you must go to David McKibbin and Eugene P. Jorgensen who supplied the unpublished letters of Sergeant Edwin J. Munn. Bonnie Sines, Department of Geography at the University of Northern Iowa, did the maps —*and* gave me a swell dog. John Johnson and Robert Martin, Department of History at the University of Northern Iowa, were supportive from the start of the project. Judy Dohlman did much of the work on the early manuscript editions and John Fink (Mahatma Johnny) helped on those editions as well. A very special expression of gratitude goes to Carole Shelley Yates who edited the final manuscripts, to Cynthia Sweet for her research on Christiana Trumbull, and to Clark Kenyon of the Camp Pope Bookshop for both publishing the book and for the cover design. Another special thank you goes to the Grateful Dead and the Quicksilver Messenger Service for typing music.

Kenneth L. Lyftogt

Introduction

While doing research for my book *From Blue Mills to Columbia: Cedar Falls and the Civil War* (Iowa State University Press 1993), I came to know a Union officer from Iowa named Matthew Mark Trumbull, captain of the Butler County Union Guards. Trumbull, known as "the hero of the Hatchie," was a minor character in the Blue Mills book, but the research led me to a remarkable article by Ray Boston of the University of Illinois-Urbana.

Boston's article is titled "General Matthew Mark Trumbull, Respectable Radical" (*Journal of Illinois History,* 66, Summer 1973). The title was rather daring given the year of the publication. By 1973 the word "radical" had become closely identified with the violent, communist/anarchist element of the anti-Vietnam War movement, which had little respectability. Yet Professor Boston's use of the term was quite deliberate. Trumbull, from his youth to his death, lived the life of a radical, but he was always an honorable man: a man to respect.

Professor Boston based much of his article on Matthew Trumbull's book, *Articles and Discussions on the Labor Question* (Chicago: Open Court Pub, Co., 1890), one of the great forgotten works of American literature. Boston's rediscovery of the book is a worthy contribution in itself.

Trumbull devoted the first forty-one pages of his book to a brief autobiography. His is the story of an American immigrant, a man who came to this country with little more than his physical strength and an eagerness to work, learn, and better himself. Within ten years of his arrival in America, he had become a lawyer—the first lawyer in Butler County, Iowa. Two years later he became the first elected representative of that county to the state legislature, and two years after that he was a captain in the Union Army. By the end of the war, Trumbull held the rank of brevet brigadier general. In his later years, he was a respected author and lecturer.

The rest of Trumbull's book contains essays, debates, and poetry that concern the great labor issues of the late 19th century: the role of unions, the question of wages, as well as debates over socialism, anarchism, and revolution. Writing under the pen name "Wheelbarrow," Trumbull writes in the tradition of Mark Twain and Will Rogers, a likable old crank who tells instructive stories.

Boston's article emphasized Trumbull as an old man who had once been a proud abolitionist and Union officer. But Boston gave little attention to Trumbull as a citizen of Iowa or his participation in the war. Trumbull himself only briefly mentioned his Civil War service in his short autobiography, but his is a story worth telling, an important part of Iowa's part in the war.

Trumbull was one of a generation of young men who were just beginning to take their places in the leadership of the state when the war came. They would become Iowa's officers—idealistic and ambitious.

Trumbull's story is also a story of the Third Iowa Volunteer Infantry, one of the state's first regiments. The Third Iowa Infantry served from the earliest campaigns of the war to the very last. This regiment gave Iowa its next governor, a lieutenant governor, and officers of many future regiments. Trumbull's story is also a story of the Ninth Iowa Volunteer Cavalry, the last cavalry regiment from Iowa—a regiment with a tragic story that has never been told.

Foreword

Chris Rossi, director of Humanities Iowa, read this portion of an article by Matthew Trumbull as part of Iowa Public Radio's series "Voices of Humanities Iowa." In the article, Trumbull linked the poetry of Scotland's Robert Burns with the politics of Thomas Jefferson to explain what he had found as an American immigrant and why it had been worth fighting for.

A Man's A Man For A' That

In his ideal of a social democracy we find the political ethics of Robert Burns. The key to it may be found in that manliest of democratic songs, "A man's a man for a' that." Here "sense and worth" are exalted as the only patents of nobility that can give legitimate rank or titles to any man. In the political morality of this song, the man who is worth the most is the man who is the most worth. It is the proud assertion of a laborer that he is a man for all that, and it is a dignified protest that shall stand forever against the degradation of "honest poverty." The political economy of it is the right of every man that every other man shall work. He must do something by hand or brain useful to the community.

I have heard this song criticized according to the canons of literary taste and style.…Let him criticize it who has toiled in the field, the factory, or the shop; him who has earned his honest bread up on the giddy mast, or down in the dark mine. As well criticize the Declaration of Independence for its rhetoric. In fact, "A man's a man for a' that," is the American Declaration of Independence condensed into the poetry of Scotland. The inspiration and the doctrine of both productions is the equality of man. I have seen the Declaration of Independence very severely criticized not only for its diction but for its politics too. I have seen fifty thousand critics in a line criticizing it with shot and shell and musketry. What of it? When their criticism ended the flag born of the declaration streamed above their speechless cannon, and from every star in its brilliant constellation there shone upon the world the gospel of the political new testament: "All men are created equal;" "A man's a man for a' that."[1]

CHAPTER 1

The Chartist

Matthew Mark Trumbull was born in the city of Westminster, St. Margaret's Parish, London County, England, in December 1826. He was born at midnight, the evil hour, and every aspect of his birth seemed to cause controversy. In his autobiography, Trumbull put it this way:

> It is a perilous thing for a man to be born at midnight, literally between two days, so that he can never have a birthday, nor tell how old he is. Besides, think of the evil auguries connected with low twelve, "when the churchyards yawn," when disembodied spirits walk the earth for punishment, when mischief broods in the time and elfish goblins hide in careless babies who trespass into the world at that unlucky hour.[1]

His mother said that he had been born on the 30th, but his father said the birth was actually past midnight on the 31st. Their disagreement was settled by the attending doctor who said that the baby was born on the very instant of midnight "and consequently not properly born at all."[2]

The next difficulty was his actual place of birth. The dividing line between St. John's and St. Margaret's parishes "ran through my father's house and lengthwise along my mother's bed. . ." so both parishes claimed the child. The whole neighborhood argued about it until they decided to toss a coin.

> The story goes that the rector of St. John won the toss, and at once decided that I was in the other parish. In this way he relieved himself of all responsibility on my account, and threw the whole burden on St. Margaret.[3]

When his parents had him baptized, the question of Trumbull's birthday came up again. This time the rector of St. Margaret ruled that he was actually born on Friday, the 30th of December.

Even his name presented problems. He was named Mark after his father and given Matthew as a middle name in honor of his uncle Matthew. But Mark — Matthew is in the wrong "apostolic order." Trumbull wrote it was "something like the Lord's Prayer backwards" that could bring a lifetime of bad luck. The name order was reversed and he became Matthew Mark Trumbull.

It is not wonderful that a boy started on a journey through the world amid contentions about the date of his birth, the place where he was born, and destined never to know his own name, should have a checkered career, embarrassed and impeded by contradictions, doubts, discords, and denials.[4]

Trumbull's parents were working class poor and very religious, "Their lives never deviated a hair's breath from the straight lines of truth, honesty, and charity."[5] His father ran a small store, but when Matthew was three years old, his father was put into the infamous Marshalsea prison as a debtor. His mother managed to borrow enough money to pay off her husband's debts and get him out of prison. "My parents sacrificed everything to pay every man his claim to the last penny, and then began the world again with nothing but stout hearts and willing hands."[6]

His parents' poverty meant that the young Matthew had to go to work. The early years of 19th century England were ones of social and economic upheaval as the Industrial Revolution took hold of the economy. The early factory system was a wage-slave system that was often brutal and unjust, trapping children from birth in poverty, misery, and degradation. Such conditions produced class antagonisms that were as bitter and hateful as any between master and slave. Trumbull was one of those children, and he nursed a resentment for the rest of his life:

Sixteen hours a day of hard work is bad schooling for a boy....In the bright days of childhood, when the mind and body should grow to strength and beauty, mine were being stunted and warped by toil savage and unnatural. I ought to be five feet ten; that's my correct stature by rights; I am less than five feet six. Toil stunted me when I was in the gristle. I had no time to study books, and the principles of life that I learned, such as they were, I had to gather in the college of hard knocks.[7]

The new economy, with its hardships, produced a many-sided reform movement that slowly gained influence in England. The movement had two great victories. The first was the Great Reform Bill of 1832, which rewarded middle-class investors and industrialists with the vote (but not the working poor). The other was the success of the English abolitionist movement. Slavery, in England proper had been abolished in 1772. In 1807, after years of being the world's leading slave-trade nation, the English Parliament (in cooperation with the U.S. government) voted to take England out of the African slave trade. In 1833 Parliament finally outlawed slavery across the empire. Slavery ended by government decree set an example for the abolition movement in America.

One of the most important parts of the reform movement in England was the struggle over what was known as Chartism. Chartism was a practical "knife and fork" movement dedicated to the idea that social equality could be achieved through political reform by finishing what the Great Reform Bill of 1832 had begun — giving the poor access to political power. Chartist reform took two forms. The first was to put pressure on Parliament's members to enact as law the six points of *The People's Charter*. The second was to go beyond political lobbying and into "direct action," a nebulous phrase that implied Jacobin-like revolution. The Peoples' Charter itself was no *Communist Manifesto;* it made no claims of historical inevitability. Nor was it a "Declaration of Independence" as it had no appeals to "nature's God" and no call to revolution. Rather, it had only political reforms that Chartists believed could transform the nation. The Chartist demands were:

1. Equal representation in Parliament.
    England should be divided into political districts with each district represented by an equal number of representatives.

2. Universal manhood suffrage.
    Every man of twenty-one years of age be entitled to vote. (Some Chartists also advocated women's suffrage as well.)

3. Annual meetings of Parliament, with a general election every year.

4. No property qualifications for members of Parliament.

5. Vote by secret ballot.

6. Regular meetings of Parliament, and pay for members of Parliament.

A Chartist demonstration in London

The center of the movement was a nationwide campaign to collect signatures on the Charter and present it to Parliament. Chartist organizers took the petition to workers in sweatshops, factories, mines, and cottage industries, and to laborers on the docks. The Chartists sponsored large public demonstrations and published a widely read journal, *The Northern Star*. Matthew Trumbull was one of many angry, idealistic young people who earned their radical's service stripes in the Chartist movement.

> At the time I speak of, the lines of caste were sharply drawn in England, and I was duly instructed to "fear God, Honor the King, and be contented in that station of life which it had pleased God to give me."...
>
> When the facts of our lives are considered it will not be surprising that we ceased to honor the King or to fear God. We became Chartists. The years of my youth were the years of the Chartist movement in England, and I flung myself headlong into it. Its high purpose, and its delirious enthusiasm attracted me. Its revolutionary promises fascinated the disenfranchised and the poor. We were ready to storm the Tower of London as the Frenchmen stormed the Bastille. I made imitation Jacobin speeches, bombastic as the real ones, and I wrote red poetry for the *Northern Star,* the fiery organ of the Chartist party.[8]

The first Charter petition, launched in Birmingham in 1838, contained 1,280,000 signatures and was presented to Parliament by a large enthusiastic crowd. The conservative members of Parliament ignored the crowd and rejected the Charter.[9]

The Chartists refused to give up and gathered even more signatures. In 1842 the Charter was again presented to Parliament. This time the Charter had 3,317,702 signatures and thousands in the streets expected passage. Yet, once again, Parliament refused to endorse the Charter.[10]

Inevitably, failure of the Charter destroyed the movement. Parliament's refusal to consider the reforms caused the more moderate supporters to abandon the Charter and allowed the more radical "direct action" members to dominate what was left of Chartism. The "direct action" Chartists became involved in more violent rhetoric and demonstrations, and some openly called for members to arm themselves. Increased Chartist radicalism resulted in increased government repression. Chartist leaders were brought to trial in the 1840s on charges of riot, conspiracy, and sedition. Three leaders were sentenced to death (but were pardoned after ten years in prison), and many others were imprisoned or transported to the English penal colonies.

The young Matthew Trumbull was not in a leadership position as a Chartist and was not threatened with either prison or deportation, but the failure of the Charter meant that he had little reason to stay in England.

> One Sunday evening I was at a coffeehouse in London where the Chartists used to meet and study the *Northern Star*. The paper for that week contained a copy of the new Constitution of Wisconsin, which territory was then making preparations for

admission as a state into the American Union. Discussing it, one of the party said, "Here is a land where the Charter is already the law; where there is plenty of work and good wages for all; why not go there?" To me the question sounded logical; if the Charter was not to be obtained in England, why not go to America, where people were all happy under its encouragement and protection! Shortly after that, I was on board an emigrant ship a-sailing Westward, Ho.[11]

CHAPTER 2

My Light Is None the Less for Lighting My Neighbor

The story of an American immigrant is always the story of a person who has strong reasons for fleeing one country and equally strong reasons for choosing to go to another country. For Trumbull those reasons were resentment and ambition. He very much resented the class structure of his native England. He resented being looked down upon as a "commoner" when he knew that he was as good a man as any. And Trumbull was ambitious. He knew that he was capable of accomplishing much, if allowed an opportunity. America was the land of opportunity.

> It was the year of the great exodus from Ireland (1846), when I bought a steerage ticket on board the pestilential *Julius Caesar*, a worm-eaten old tub bound from Liverpool to Quebec. She was in the lumber trade, and her scheme was to take out a cargo of emigrants, and bring back a cargo of lumber....The crazy old vessel was crowded with rats, a phenomenon I could not understand. What pleasure or comfort they could find in that ship was always a mystery to me.[1]

The cross-Atlantic voyage was a horror. Trumbull described the "dark, damp, and noisome dungeon called the 'hold'" crowded with over four hundred desperate men, women, and children, "mostly Irish peasant farmers and their families, fleeing from the famine which was then ravaging Ireland."[2]

The passengers were told that the crossing would take about three weeks but, to be safe, the ship carried supplies for a month. The supplies turned out to be foul water and hard bread that was "black, moldy, and full of worms." Typhus and dysentery broke out in the crowded hold before the ship was a week out to sea. On the eighth day, a young Irishman died and was "flung into the sea without preparation or prayer." Storms tore the sails, broke the masts, and spoiled much of the dry bread, and death became a daily thing on what proved to be a fifty-five day ordeal. Trumbull described the voyage.

> There was a rugged Englishman on board....His mother was with him, a ministering angel, always comforting the sick. She took fever and died. When we buried her in the sea the stalwart Englishman went mad. There was a peasant farmer with us from the south of Ireland, accompanied by his wife and three children. They were kind, respectable people, and the children were good looking and good. One

18

of them, a bright little boy about seven years old, was my particular playmate and pet. One day the fever struck him and speedily burned him to death. We placed him on the floor underneath the hatchway for the advantage of such fresh air as might be thereby obtained. While his father and mother knelt in agony beside him, watching his throbbing pulses beating fainter and fainter, until they stopped forever. The photograph of that scene is imprinted on my memory ineffaceable evermore. In a few days another of the children died, and then the last one. When wè landed at Grosse Isle (Canada), I saw the father and mother, fever smitten and delirious, swung ashore in baskets.[3]

The fever struck passengers and crew alike; even the captain of the ship fell victim. Trumbull was spared, he believed, because he refused to live in the hold of the ship. Instead he and a half a dozen others took refuge in the ship's longboat and slept amid the "ropes, blocks, tackle, and miscellaneous rubbish." They were exposed to wind and rain but also to more fresh air than the other passengers and Trumbull believed "that in my case it operated as an antidote to the deadly 'ship-fever.'" He summed up the voyage with these words:

> No regiment in the civil war could show such a list of killed and wounded in any battle, or in any two or three battles, as our little regiment could show as the result of a fifty-five days campaign on board the *Julius Caesar.*[4]

The *Julius Caesar* was not permitted to land in Quebec but was sent to the nearby Grosse Isle, a quarantine ground. The healthy Trumbull was immediately given work as a roustabout unloading ships filled with lumber to be used in making sheds for the hundreds of sick immigrants from the *Julius Caesar* and other ships. A few days later a steamboat took him and the other healthy passengers to Quebec, but, again, Quebec authorities refused to let them enter. The steamboat then took the passengers to Montreal and dumped them on the levee. Others might have felt helpless and abandoned, but not Trumbull. He soon discovered that he had found exactly what he wanted when he shipped out of Liverpool, honest work in America.

> ...the new world already looked bright and beautiful. Men were actually walking about the levee inviting the newly come emigrants to work. I saw in a moment that it was only a question of health and strength with me, and that I need not be hungry in America.[5]

Trumbull was given work on a railroad construction gang near the St. Lawrence River for a dollar a day. It was here that he acquired an important skill and the pen name that he would use in the future —"Wheelbarrow." Wheeling a barrow full of dirt up a plank efficiently took a great deal of practice. It was a "skill" that Trumbull and his fellow workers took very seriously. In fact, they were so serious that Trumbull and many others refused to help newcomers learn how to do it, thinking that this made their skill more valuable. Over this small issue, Trumbull learned one of the most important lessons of his life:

> One day a greenhorn came along and got a job on our gang; he was awkward as a landlubber trying to climb the top-gallantmast. He would look at his feet as he went up the plank, and the wheel of the "barrow" would run off; he would look at the wheel and his feet would step off; he asked advice, but we who had learned the trade had now become monopolists, and refused to give any instruction; all of us except Jemmy Hill; he took the fellow in hand and showed him how to walk the plank, which he obviously had no right to do. That night, up at the shanty where we lived, my tongue swaggered a good deal, to the admiration of everybody except Jemmy Hill....
>
> The next day was Sunday, and Jemmy and I took a walk to a favorite spot where we used to smoke our pipes and gossip. The glorious St. Lawrence rolled at our feet, and the sun shone bright overhead. Jemmy was a young fellow from the north of Ireland, about five feet nine or ten, slim, all sinew and bone, blue eyes, light and fair, smooth face, beautiful as a girl's. He had a soft musical voice, and there was nothing manly about him, except that he liked to smoke; but he was as brave as Phil Sheridan; he was a holy terror in a fight; I saw him scatter a dozen fellows once in a riot, like Samson used to clear out those Philistines. He is president of a railroad now, and rides in his own special car, in which there is always a berth for me.
>
> We talked about the necessity of protecting our craft from "plug" workmen, or, rather, I did; Jemmy merely smoked his pipe and listened. At last he pulled out of his pocket a watch-charm, and handed it to me to examine. The crest on it was a couple of torches, one lighting the other, with this motto underneath: "My light is none the less for lighting my neighbor." He explained that this was the motto of some secret society that he belonged to in Belfast; I forget the name of it now, but no matter, that was the motto of it. "My light is none the less for lighting my neighbor." I accepted the rebuke and acknowledged that the motto was a good one. That was many years ago but the longer I live the more I am convinced that it is sound in political science and social economy.[6]

After working on the railroad for a few months and managing to save a little money, Trumbull left the construction gang and set off on foot for the United States. He had lived his entire life in the shadows and soot of London and now the vast forests and open roads of America were a delight. While on the road near Granby, Canada, a local farmer offered Trumbull work. Not being a man to turn down work and wages, he took the job. He soon discovered that farming is also "skilled labor" and that he was no good at it: "I could not learn to milk, to chop, to pitch hay, or do anything else."[7] His failure at farming led to his next opportunity in America. His employer saw that the young man was no farmer but, rather than sending him down the road, he told Trumbull that the little community needed a school teacher and he would recommend Trumbull for the job.

The offer amazed Trumbull. He had never had much schooling in England but he had learned to write very well and was willing to study hard and learn the rest. He got the job and for the rest of that fall and winter he boarded with different Granby farmers and taught in their district school.

> I was treated with unbounded hospitality. Among the happiest portions of my life was the winter when I taught school and "boarded round" among the hospitable settlers in the backwoods of Canada.
>
> And now for the first time I tasted the luxuries of an intellectual life. My work was light, and improving to the mind. It was more educational to me than to the pupils.
>
> My term having expired, I resumed the march to Boston. My exalted position at Granby had awakened within me a new ambition, and I felt the throbbings of a higher aspiration. I had been advised at Granby by a friendly patron to study the law. At first I thought he was jesting, but he was entirely serious, and he assured me that the professions in America were not as in England, the exclusive property of the rich. The dream was a fascination, for I was anxious to escape the drudgery of the shovel and the wheelbarrow. [8]

Trumbull did not mention that while in Canada he met a young woman about fifteen years old named Christiana. She became Mrs. Matthew Trumbull and, when the school year was over and he "resumed the march to Boston," Christiana was with him.[9]

The two made their way to Boston with Trumbull stopping along the way to do wheelbarrow work on the railroads. When they got to Boston the only work he could get was in a pork warehouse handling huge barrels of salted pork for a dollar a day. It was hard work but lighter than railroad work and for Trumbull "The skies were getting brighter and brighter every day."[10]

It was the spring of 1847 and the United States was at war with Mexico. One day Trumbull passed a recruiting station and enlisted, simply because "…there was excitement, adventure, and foreign travel, all to be had for nothing."[11]

It was a controversial war. Many Americans, especially Northern abolitionists, saw the war as part of a Southern attempt to gain more land for cotton and slaves. Congressman Abraham Lincoln opposed the war. The philosopher Henry David Thoreau spent his famous night in jail for refusing to pay his taxes to support the war. Also the young officer U. S. Grant, in spite of serving heroically in the war, always believed that the bloodshed of the Civil War was God's punishment to the country for its invasion of Mexico.

Trumbull served for less than a year, rising from private to first sergeant in the 2nd U.S. Artillery, and seeing action in the battles of Palo Alto, Monterey, and Chapultapec. Trumbull wrote nothing of the particulars of his part in the war but he, too, came to condemn the war.

> Before I had been a soldier two hours, my enthusiasm for conquering people received a shock from which it has never entirely recovered. I happened to pick up a newspaper which contained a sarcastic poem about the war. It was written by Hosea Bigelow....One verse oppressed me like a nightmare, and it weights on my conscience still. This was the verse:
>
> > "If you take a sword and dror it"
> > And should stick a feller thro;'
> > Guv'ment aint to answer for it,
> > God will send the bill to you."
>
> I believe the sentiment of that verse is based on moral truth, but I believe that when a set of men called "Government" plunge nations into war, they will have to answer for it, and that God will send the bill to them....
>
> Of course, I knew nothing at that time of the ethics or the politics of the war with Mexico; but afterwards, when I came to study the genius and inspiration of it, I thought it nothing to be proud of; unless we regard the acquisition of California and New Mexico as a great achievement. That must be considered a valuable result, if we leave out of the estimate the moral quality by which it was obtained.[12]

After his discharge from the Army, Trumbull and his wife traveled along the East Coast from Boston to Virginia. Trumbull worked at many jobs but did not forget his ambition of studying law. While working in Norfolk, Virginia, Trumbull made friends with a lawyer who helped with the necessary study of Latin, lent him books, and gave him unofficial instruction.

From Norfolk they moved Richmond, Virginia, and, in 1850, Christiana gave birth to their first child, a son. They named him Matthew Mark, in the correct "apostolic order."[13] Life in Richmond, the Paris of the American South, was very good. Trumbull worked at a series of jobs and continued to study law in the evenings and Christiana made a home for them and their baby. All might have gone well except for Trumbull's "imprudent habit" of criticizing the Southern institution of human slavery. For him, slavery was the ultimate example of how far workers could be degraded.

> One Sunday I was taking a walk with a friend of mine in Richmond, and I remarked upon the inequality of the negroes in the streets, as indicated by their personal appearance. Some were ragged, brutal faced, and twisted out of shape by premature and unnatural toil; others were well clad and evidently well fed. One bright mulatto, of genteel figure and face, was clad in black broadcloth; he wore

a shiny silk-hat and carried a cane. It was easy to see that there were castes among them, superiors and inferiors, and that the higher order looked with scorn on the lower classes. I thought that those finely dressed negroes were probably free. "No," said my friend, "They are all slaves, but there are degrees in slavery; there are 'soft things' there as in freedom."

The next day I was standing at the Washington monument, when I saw a procession of negroes fastened by couples to a long chain. They were marching to the shambles to be sold, where I followed them to see the auction. That lot of fellow-Christians brought, on average, about six dollars a pound. Among them was the bright mullato—plug hat, broadcloth and all. He was chained to a vulgar looking field hand. All supercilious airs were gone, and every face carried the same look of hopeless despair. All distinctions were leveled in the handcuffs that tightened them to a common chain.[14]

The white citizens of Richmond were thrown into terror in 1852 when a house slave named Jane Williams killed her mistress, Mrs. Joseph P. Winston, and the Winston baby as the two slept. Rumors quickly spread that the Winston killings were the signal for a full-scale urban revolution by Richmond's slaves.

Jane Williams was put on trial for her life and the trial became a public spectacle. The court house was crowded with spectators every day while self-styled militia units paraded through streets that were already crowded with drunken toughs bent on terrorizing the city's blacks and any known enemies of slavery. Jane Williams was convicted of murder and sentenced to hang. Over nine thousand white citizens watched her die on the Richmond gallows.[15]

Trumbull knew that Richmond was no place for him or his family:

When the Winston family was murdered by a female slave, a panic struck the town of Richmond, for the people thought it the signal for a negro insurrection, and a search for Abolitionists was immediately organized; something like a wolf hunt. I was not curious to see the end of it, and that night found me in Fredericksburg. The next morning I was in Washington. From there I started westward, and did not stop until I was landed safely on the free soil of the western prairies.[16]

CHAPTER 3

Iowa

The "free soil of the western prairies" meant Iowa. Trumbull, Christiana, and Matthew Jr. were one of many families who crossed the Mississippi River by ferryboat and found themselves in "the beautiful land." Iowa was a young state, admitted to the Union in 1846, a pioneer state where an ambitious man could make his mark. By the terms of the Missouri Compromise of 1820, Iowa was a state that was off limits to slavery.

Railroads had not yet made their way to Iowa so Trumbull could not get work at his wheelbarrow trade. However, he managed to get a job in a brickyard near Cedar Rapids. He also continued to pursue his ambition to be a lawyer. He again sought out a friendly lawyer who loaned him books and gave him serious training, including regular examinations.

Brick making was a seasonal job that ended with the first frost, and Trumbull found himself out of work again. He then turned to his teaching experience and he secured a winter position teaching school. During the winter of 1852-1853 he also studied seriously to pass the Iowa bar. At the same time Trumbull continued to teach himself literature, math, and grammar so that he could better teach his students.

That spring (1853) he was admitted to the Iowa bar, but the exam wasn't easy. Trumbull wrote that it was ". . .an unusually severe examination, caused by prejudice of the bar against the admission of a brick-yard laborer."[1]

Lawyer or not, he still had a family to support and Trumbull was forced to go back to work in the brickyard:

> I was great sport for the other fellows in the brick-yard, and they always called me "counselor." With grave pleasantry the boss would say: "Will the learned counsel on the other side bring more clay?"...I enjoyed this banter more than they did because it was based on fact, and was a prophecy of better times for me.[2]

He worked long enough at the brickyard to save money to purchase the needed books for his legal library and to move to another part of the state because "...I well knew it would be useless to open a law office among people who had seen me working in a brick-yard."[3]

In the fall of 1853, Trumbull and his family found their Iowa home in the town of Clarksville, the newly established county seat of Butler County near the Cedar and Shell Rock Rivers in Northeast Iowa. The town was named for the Clark family. Thomas Clark had built one of the first cabins in the area, and Abner Clark had opened the first dry goods store. The town was platted in August 1853 and consisted of twenty-three blocks, not including the county courthouse blocks, with a new courthouse building and city square. There was a post office, new stores, a livery stable, and a dam and race that brought water to a mill. The town seemed ready to become the key trading center in the upper Cedar Valley. Trumbull and his family took a house on South Main Street and he opened the county's first law office.[4]

In the early summer of 1854 the towns in the upper Cedar Valley received reports that Indians were on the warpath. Northeast Iowa was thrown into a panic. Trumbull and the rest of the pioneers were eastern people who had been brought up on stories of the deadly warriors of the prairies and they took the reports very seriously. (Such fears were not totally unfounded. Iowa was on the frontier and occasional violent skirmishes occurred between Indians and the settlers; the Spirit Lake Massacre happened just three years later.) Hundreds of people from Butler and Bremer Counties fled south to the town of Cedar Falls, or even as far down the valley as Cedar Rapids. Trumbull took his family to Cedar Falls but refused to go any further.

Abner Eads, superintendent of public instruction for Iowa and a veteran of the Mexican War, happened to be visiting Cedar Falls at the time. When the town filled

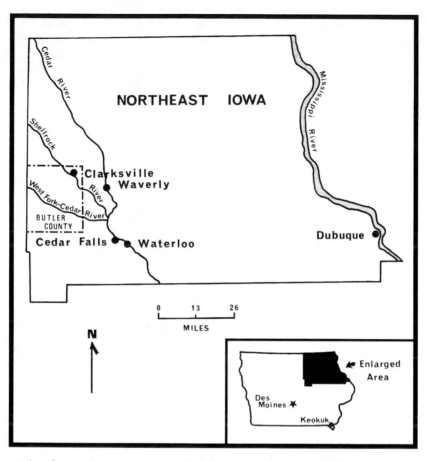

up with refugees, he immediately called for volunteers to march back up the valley and rescue the settlers who did not get away. One of the first volunteers was Matthew M. Trumbull, eager to get back to Clarksville. Eads was elected colonel and Trumbull was given the title adjutant-general and chief of staff. Two companies of dragoons were organized. One was officially from Black Hawk County under Captain Edwin Brown, and the other from Bremer County under Captain Jerry Farris, but volunteers from Butler County were in both companies. Eads and Trumbull did their best to give the men some sort of experience in military drill, and, after a couple of days of preparation, they took their men north. The long column reached Clarksville after a hard forced march and made their first night's camp just outside of town. The terrified citizens who had stayed in town cheered their rescuers and eagerly emptied their cupboards and pantries to feed the soldiers.

The next day Colonel Eads left some of his men in Clarksville with orders to build a defensible fort on one of the nearby hills. The troops immediately named the place Fort Eads and started to work digging ditches and felling trees. They worked with a fury fully expecting an attack at any time. Colonel Eads and Trumbull then mounted their horses and led the rest of their men towards Clear Lake and the waiting savages. (Sometime during his years in America Trumbull had become a proficient horseman.)

Later that day the march was halted when some settlers from the west met the column and informed Eads and Trumbull that the whole story was wrong. Two Winnebago Indians had been murdered by a band of other Indians near the Minnesota border but there had been no attacks on white people, and no war parties raiding into the valley. Colonel Eads turned his troops back. During the trip back, the men, who had carefully saved their ammunition for an Indian fight, took to letting off steam by shooting at stuff along the road. The gunfire, however, panicked the settlers who stayed on their farms. They thought the fighting had started and took off for Clarksville and Fort Eads. Their arrival further upset the volunteers at the fort and the people left in Clarksville who had not yet heard of the false alarm.

That night the men of the two volunteer companies made camp again in Clarksville near the newly constructed trenches and earthworks of the fort. They were still nervous, afraid that the Indian story was the truth, very tired, and feeling a bit foolish if the story was not true. With these things in mind, Chief of Staff Trumbull went off to bathe in the river. When he got there he saw a farm woman calmly doing the family wash in the waters of the Shell Rock, the only sensible person he had seen. Trumbull always liked a joke, even a poor one, and he decided to cry wolf. Just as the men were settling in for the night he came running back from his bath shouting that there were thousands of Indians on the other side of the river. The 1883 *History of Butler County* said this about Trumbull's prank:

> The bold soldiers were off in a trice, not toward the enemy but each on his own hook bound toward the protecting walls of the little fortification. There timid women wrung their hands and fainted while the children wept. Quietude was at length restored; a hearty laugh was indulged in; the war was ended and all returned to their peaceful homes. Thus closed the Indian Massacre of 1854.[5]

The Indian scare and short-lived militia companies became a part of the folklore of the Cedar Valley. In 1929 the Clarksville American Legion placed a brass plaque on a small boulder at the corner of Adams and Superior Streets in Clarksville marking the site of Fort Eads.

With the Indian war over Trumbull and his family settled into life in Clarksville. He gained the reputation as a lawyer who was willing to take cases that involved poorer people in disputes with creditors, but he was also friend and lawyer to George

Poisal, the wealthiest man in town. The 1883 *History of Butler County* contains this story of the two men (though Trumbull is inaccurately called "General" long before he had earned the rank):

> General Trumbull, when he first came to Butler County, was a man of more than ordinary ability....He was a kind, generous-hearted man, of good impulses and a great deal of integrity....
>
> General Trumbull had no difficulty making friends and once made they were fast and sincere. George Poisal and Mr. Trumbull were intimate friends and often had law business to transact. One day in April, 1857, George came into Trumbull's office, and in the course of conversation, remarked, that he had just received a new litter of pigs. "Well," says the General, "that's just what I want. You had better give me one of them!" "All right;" answers George; "you shall have one." The matter ran along for some months, and nothing was said about it. Finally one day in November, George again chanced to be in the General's office and stated that he had just killed a lot of fatted hogs. "By the way," remarked Trumbull, "I just happened to think of it. How is that hog you gave me, doing?" "That hog," exclaimed Poisal, "that's the very litter I've been killing. You never called for it." "Well," Trumbull answers, "I thought the matter over, and decided to let you fat it on shares." A general laugh was indulged in, and the following morning a fine dressed porker was sent to the General's house."[6]

As his law practice grew, so did Trumbull's family. Christiana gave birth to a second son, Peter, in 1855, and in 1857, a third son, Charles.[7]

The ambitious Trumbull soon discovered that he had political talents. Over ten years away from his English Chartism, Trumbull was still a radical and easily found a place in the new Republican Party. It was a "free soil" party determined to prevent the expansion of slavery, and it was a worker's party that championed such ideas as the Homestead Acts. Its slogan was "Free Soil, Free Labor, Free Men!" — principles that were dear to Trumbull.

Trumbull was thrust into the political arena by the financial panic of 1857. Just as it seemed that Iowa was on the brink of prosperity, the state suddenly went broke. The problem began outside of Iowa, which had no independent banking system. Iowa financiers were forced to depend on out-of-state banks that set up branch offices in Iowa. The branch banks manufactured a variety of paper bills and Iowans had no choice; they had to use the bills. As long as the out-of-state banks were sound, the system worked (not very well, but it sufficed). But in 1857 the out-of-state banks failed, so their Iowa branches also failed. Benjamin F. Gue, a Fort Dodge Republican member of the 1858 state legislature and later one of Iowa's finest historians, described the situation this way:

> Thousands of citizens were unable to get money to pay taxes or to save their property from sale under the summary process of deeds of trust from which there was

no redemption at the time. Thousands were reduced from prosperous farmers, merchants and mechanics to poverty and destitution.[8]

Small towns such as Clarksville were almost stopped dead by the crisis and Trumbull, with his reputation as a tribune of the working man, was persuaded to run for office:

> My objection to office holding did not last long, and in the fall of 1857, I was nominated on the republican ticket for the legislature. There were three counties in the district and the political battle was fought all over them. After a bitter contest I was elected; and in the following January I took my seat as a member of the House.[9]

Trumbull's service in the state legislature brought him into contact with many of the men who would soon play important roles in Iowa's part in the Civil War. The most important of these men was Samuel Jordan Kirkwood, newly elected to the State Senate. Kirkwood, a true "free soil" man and Iowa City farmer, was one of the founders of Iowa's Republican Party and one of its leading voices. He later became Iowa's governor during the Civil War. His office determined the policies that guided the state and the commissions of Iowa's officers would be signed by him.[10]

Also in the State Senate was Mississippi-born Aaron Brown. Brown, like many Southerners, hated slavery and came north to Fayette County, Iowa, where he became one of the leaders of the abolitionist wing of the new Republican Party. When the war came, Brown led a company of Fayette County volunteers and served alongside Matthew Trumbull.[11]

Another important man served in the Iowa House. The previously mentioned Benjamin F. Gue was also an out and out abolitionist and one of the Iowa's earliest Republicans.[12]

Also in the House was Thomas Drummond, from Vinton. Drummond was a Virginia-born Iowan, another Southern-born enemy of slavery. He was editor of the *Vinton Eagle* and earned a reputation as a hard drinking, combative Republican who generally got what he wanted. Drummond was the man who brought the State School for the Blind to Vinton. When the war came, Drummond left politics and joined Iowa's 4th Volunteer Cavalry where he served with distinction. Later he became a captain in the regular U.S. Army (5th Cavalry) and was killed in the Battle of Five Forks, Virginia, the decisive battle that led directly to the capture of the Confederate capital of Richmond.[13]

William W. Belknap was elected to the House from Keokuk as a Democrat but switched parties when the war came. He joined the Army and earned a reputation for heroism from Shiloh to Atlanta. After the war Belknap served for seven years as President U. S. Grant's secretary of war only to disgrace the Grant presidency by getting caught up in a series of financial scandals that contributed to the image of Grant as a failed president.[14]

Zimri Streeter, from Black Hawk County, was the grandfather of Bess Streeter Aldrich, one of Iowa's most respected authors. (He served as the model for the character of Jeremiah Martin in her novel *Song of Years.*) Streeter was one of Iowa's true log cabin pioneers. At fifty-nine years old his younger fellow members in the House affectionately called him "Old Black Hawk." Streeter was another early "free soil" Republican but he was a hard-nosed economic conservative who often clashed with radicals such as Trumbull.[15]

The most important Democrat to serve with Trumbull in the state legislature was Dennis A. Mahoney from Dubuque. Mahoney, editor of the *Dubuque Herald,* was the most outspoken anti-war voice in Iowa. He used his newspaper and his political office to oppose the war. President Lincoln in 1862 had Mahoney arrested and hauled off to prison in Washington D.C. for three months without a trial. Mahoney's case is often cited as precedent for a commander-in-chief's right to ignore civil rights during time of war.[16]

The 1858 Iowa Legislature was one of the most important in the state's history. It was the first session to meet in the new capitol building in Des Moines, a frontier city of fewer than 3,000 people with newly planted trees lining muddy streets. Des Moines was also suffering under the economic crisis. Many vacant lots could not be sold because no one was building, and other buildings that once held busy stores and businesses were vacant. The start of the new session with the influx of out-of-towners who needed to be housed, fed, and entertained was a needed economic relief.

The 1858 legislature was also the first session to meet under the new state constitution of 1857. It was a Republican document—the first great triumph of Iowa's Republicans. On the subject of slavery in Iowa it was clear: "There shall be no slavery in this state; nor shall there be involuntary servitude, unless it be for the punishment of a crime."[17]

While the new constitution forbade slavery, it retained many racially discriminatory laws from early constitutions, including denying the vote to any but white men. Such discrimination reflected the ugliest contradiction of the age: one could hate slavery yet hate the slave as well. Trumbull would later one dangerous night as a Union officer come face-to-face with the violence of that contradiction.

The 1858 Iowa Legislature did its work while the nation itself was being torn apart over the issues that turned into the Civil War. Kansas was already "bleeding" in its own civil war as "free soil" and pro-slavery militias fought over its constitution. The U.S. Supreme Court added to the problem by ruling in the Dred Scott case of 1857 that a black man had no legal standing before the courts, so living on "free soil" did not make a man free.

In 1839, the Iowa Territorial Supreme Court heard a similar case, but the results were the opposite. It was the first case heard under Chief Justice Charles Mason (the only man in Robert E. Lee's class at West Point with a better record than Lee). The Iowa court ruled in favor of a slave named Ralph who had lived on Iowa's "free soil" and, thus was a free man. However, the case was not used as a precedent by the U.S. Supreme Court in the Dred Scott case.[18] The Supreme Court went even further in its Dred Scott ruling and nullified the Compromise of 1820, taking the position that the national government never had the authority to place restrictions on slavery.

The Republican Party rejected the court's rulings and promised to appoint "free soil" judges if it captured the White House in 1860. The party found a powerful spokesman in the former Whig congressman Abraham Lincoln of Illinois. Lincoln was a former backwoods rail splitter who believed in protecting American workers. That made him popular with the common man, but he was also a successful railroad attorney and corporate lawyer and was acceptable to Northern business interests. Plus, his "free soil" position was so strong that even the abolitionists liked him.

The Republican Party had few followers in the South, and by 1858 the most powerful Southern Democrats were openly calling for secession if the Republicans ever got the White House.

Trumbull and his fellow politicians had much work to do in the 1858 state legislature. That legislative session addressed the financial crisis by passing a general banking law in the state with strict security requirements. New state banks were opened on sound financial footing and did much to end the crisis. Benjamin F. Gue, the law's chief author, writing years later as a historian, said:

> The state Banks were sound institutions, always paying their depositers in full specie and redeeming their currency whenever presented. It is probable that no better or safer banking system was ever devised, and it did the banking business of the state to the entire satisfaction of the people until superseded by the National Banks.[19]

Also in the session, the Iowa Republicans, showing their defiance of the Supreme Court and over the fierce objections of Democrats led by Dennis Mahoney, passed a resolution that condemned the Dred Scott decision, saying that the court's ruling was:

> ...not binding in law or conscience upon the government or the people of the United States...the state of Iowa will not allow slavery within her borders, in any form or under any pretext, for any time, however short, be the consequences what they may.[20]

Trumbull wrote this about the 1858 session:

> I was now an American statesman, and I played the part with perfect satisfaction to myself. The office yielded glory and renown, but not much money; for in those

days the wages for a statesman was only three dollars a day. This was better pay than I got on the railroad, or in the brick-yard, and on the railroad, a motion to adjourn was always "out of order." I acquitted myself as a statesman about as well as the rest of them....

There were some comical scenes in that legislature.... The great commercial panic occurred in 1857, and our chief statesmanship consisted in passing laws to hinder and prevent the collection of debts, especially debts due to bloated capitalists and wholesale merchants living outside the state. We needed all our money for home consumption, and we did not intend that our people should waste it paying foreign debts.... There was an old pioneer farmer there who went by the name Blackhawk, and one day when some of this generous legislation was under debate, he rose in his place and said: "Mr. Speaker! I would like to ax a question. If this yar bill passes, will it be a criminal offense for a man to pay his honest debts if he has a mind to?"[21]

(This story first appeared in a Des Moines newspaper in 1858 and was the making of Streeter's reputation as a colorful Iowa character. Streeter's friend, Peter Melendy, used it in an article on Streeter, and Bess Streeter Aldrich used it in *Song of Years*.)[22] Trumbull ended his description with one more anecdote:

An active and very influential member of the House was Tom Drummond, a bright young fellow from Benton County. He was killed in the war, fighting bravely under Sheridan at the battle of Five Forks. Tom was a fine singer, and one day, after he had spent the previous night at a convivial gathering, he got sleepy, and at last, dropping his head upon his desk, took a nap. The House went on with its business and took no notice of Tom. Waking up in the afternoon, he thought he was still at the jollification, and immediately began to sing in a clear loud voice the melody of "Auld Lang Syne." The members looked at each other in amazement, and at last they gazed at the speaker, expecting that he would order the Sergeant-at-arms to arrest the honorable member for his unparalleled breach of decorum. Instead of that the Speaker listened for a moment, and then bringing his gavel down heavily on his desk, he shouted: "The House will join in the chorus."[23]

CHAPTER 4

The Butler County Union Guards

Trumbull left the Iowa Legislature after one term and was never again elected to such an office, but the experience had been very good for him. He believed that he had done some good for his constituents, ". . . and my experience in the legislature enlarged the circle of my acquaintance with prominent men, which was of great benefit to me in a professional way."[1]

As Trumbull resumed his law practice, the country continued on its race to war. Northeast Iowa became a hotbed of Republican activity and Trumbull was one of thousands of activists dedicated to the election of Abraham Lincoln. Lincoln was elected in 1860 and, during the long lame-duck session of President James Buchanan, Southerners made good their promise of secession. South Carolina went first and by the spring of 1861 eleven states had joined the new Confederate States of America.

On 12 April 1861 Confederate artillery opened fire on Fort Sumter in Charleston Harbor, South Carolina, an open act of defiance by the South. President Lincoln responded by calling for each loyal state to do its part in raising a 75,000-man volunteer army capable of smashing the Confederacy. Iowa was to furnish a full regiment, one thousand men.

Samuel Jordan Kirkwood, elected governor of Iowa in 1860, received the news at his Coralville farm. He had served through the winter session of the legislature and by April was back home. The official telegraph from President Lincoln's Secretary of War, Simon Cameron, arrived in Davenport on 16 April 1861. (Davenport was the only Iowa city with telegraph connection to the East). The telegram read:

> To his Excellently Samuel J. Kirkwood
> Governor of Iowa
> Calls made on you by tonight's mail for one regiment of militia for immediate service.[2]

The news spread quickly across Davenport and one of those who heard it was William Vandever, a member of the U.S. House of Representatives just home from Washington D.C. Vandever boarded the first train for Iowa City, near Coralville, eager to personally deliver the message to Governor Kirkwood. Vandever, so the story goes, found Iowa's governor in his boots and overalls tending to his livestock. When

Kirkwood read the message he looked at Vandever and asked, "Why, the President wants a whole regiment of men! Do you suppose, Mr. Vandever, I can raise that many?"[3]

A day later the Governor responded to the official message with his own proclamation to the citizens of Iowa:

> Now, therefore, I, Samuel Jordan Kirkwood, Governor of the State of Iowa... hereby call upon the Militia of this State Immediately to form in the different counties, Volunteer companies with a view of entering the Active Military service of the United States....[4]

If Kirkwood was concerned about the response to his proclamation, he need not have worried. The North had not been idle from November to April; patriotism was at a fever pitch. Huge pro-Union rallies were held all across the North where fiery speakers called for war in defense of the Union, and young men stepped forward to fight. Congressman Vandever, for example, had spoken at many war rallies and proudly declared that if war came he would resign his seat in the House and become a soldier. (In August 1861 Governor Kirkwood appointed Vandever colonel of the 9th Iowa Infantry. He and his regiment had a combat record second to none and Vandever ended the war with the rank of brevet major-general.)

In the weeks following the Governor's proclamation, hundreds of ambitious and politically well-connected men from across Iowa took to calling themselves major or captain and began to organize Kirkwood's militia companies. Some of these would-be officers had experience in the Mexican War, some had served in other militia units, and many had no military experience at all. They were a diverse bunch, eager for distinction, and with one thing in common—they could inspire men to follow them. Whether or not they could lead those men into battle had yet to be proven.

On Saturday, 4 May 1861, this article appeared in the *Butler County Jeffersonian*, a Republican newspaper published in Butler Center and edited by William Haddock.

> Butler County In Arms!
> It affords me the great pleasure to be able to state that Butler County is not going to be behind her sister counties in supplying soldiers to fight for the stars and stripes. Captain Trumbull of Clarksville is now organizing a company, and its ranks are nearly filled. The captain has seen service in the Mexican War, and is well qualified in every respect to take command of a company....Young men of Butler, you will never have a better chance to serve your country than now. Our glorious Union is in danger of being destroyed—our government subverted by a horde of pro-slavery ruffians—and it is the duty of everyone who is not prevented by insuperable difficulties, to shoulder his musket and march to the support of his country. We do not apprehend that the Northern forces are going

to be much damaged in the conflict, inasmuch as it appears to be the intention of the government to overawe its enemies with superior numbers—so that those who enlist will run no danger of being killed—but even if there was a desperate risk to be encountered, every true friend of his country would be all the more eager to brave the peril. Then hasten to fill up the ranks of the Butler company. A little service will do you good—a little travel just now will brush up your knowledge of geography, and now is your time to improve opportunities, and at the same time be fed clothed and paid by the government. And if, after enlistment, you should happen to be drawn up in front of the enemy, remember that our watchword is *freedom*—theirs, *slavery*.[5]

That same Saturday night Clarksville held a war rally. Hundreds of people from across Butler County assembled on the courthouse lawn to see the first formal formation of Trumbull's company, the Butler County Union Guards. A stage was set up and decorated with flags and bunting and more flags lined the town's main street. Some of Butler County's leading citizens spoke to the cheering crowd, calling for support for the flag and the Union. Resolutions were put forth and passed in honor of all who volunteered to join Trumbull. Committees were called to gather funds for the families of the soldiers, and everyone joined in singing the "Star Spangled Banner." Matthew Trumbull was the last to speak. The old Chartist orator, Iowa lawyer, and politician knew how to inspire a crowd. As Editor Haddock wrote, "...towards the close of Trumbull's remarks the greatest enthusiasm prevailed."[6] Standing in military formation in front of the stage were twenty young men, Trumbull's first recruits, dressed in their Sunday best and carrying whatever arms they had. When Trumbull finished his speech, he proudly walked off the stage and stood in front of his men. He called them to order in his best military fashion. They snapped to attention, and he, using whatever army training he still remembered from 1847, put the men through a brief company drill, ending with a formal salute. Trumbull stood ramrod straight, accepted the salute, and then commanded the company to break ranks. The men, now on their own, assembled not far from the stage and formally elected Trumbull as their captain.[7]

Trumbull accepted the rank with great pride. He was thirty-five years old, the father of three sons, and an established community leader with a good law practice. He could have stayed home, but he didn't. He campaigned as hard for his captaincy as he had for the legislature. This was his war, the one he had fought since his Chartist youth! Trumbull and other anti-slavery Northerners hated slavery because it was the basis of an American aristocracy that not only degraded the slave but also doomed white workers to the status of "poor white trash." Trumbull's friend Henry Perkins, editor of the *Cedar Falls Gazette,* published an article in September 1861 titled "What Are We Fighting For" that very much reflected Trumbull's reasons for going to war:

Does any one for a moment suppose that if the South should be successful, it would re-establish a government like the present, like the one it is now endeavoring to destroy? If there are any such let them dismiss the thought immediately. A government founded by the slave oligarchy, with slavery as the cornerstone must, of necessity, be hostile to freedom. Mechanics, laborers, farmers, how do they speak of you today? Do they not call you serfs, white-slaves, mud-sills, and every opprobrious epithet a pampered and haughty aristocracy can invent. Should the Southern cause prevail the condition of the middle and laboring classes of the North would be on the same footing as those in Poland or Hungary.[8]

Ray Boston, of the University of Illinois-Urbana, in his 1973 article "Respectable Radical," quoted an old friend of Trumbull's who was very clear on just why the English-born Iowan went to war:

Some may have joined the army in those days simply to preserve the union of the states—not so General Trumbull. He joined the army and participated in that great conflict for the purpose of freeing the Negro....He felt that the end of the war would simultaneously be the end of slavery.[9]

Only sixteen of Trumbull's original Butler County Union Guards were from Clarksville, the rest came from Butler, Bremer, and Black Hawk Counties. Trumbull and the other self-appointed captains spent the spring of 1861 in a wide-ranging, good-natured, rivalry for volunteers. They traveled from town to town and war rally to war rally, made speeches, wrote letters, and glad-handed the right political friends. They volunteered their own funds to equip their companies, paraded their men in front of hometown audiences, and generally did all they could to whip Iowa into a fighting fury. Trumbull was one of the best. A reporter for the *Cedar Falls Gazette* describing a rally in Charles City wrote that Trumbull "...made a soul stirring speech of about thirty-minutes."[10] The *Dubuque Daily Times* reported that "...Mr. Trumbull from Butler Co. who came into the city with an offer of a hundred men, made a speech with much effect, and received great applause."[11]

Trumbull, in his brief autobiography, said little about the particulars of his war service but he said this about why he became such an eager captain:

When my legal career appeared most promising, it was rudely interrupted by the outbreak of the war. The attack on Fort Sumter was Treason's defiance to all free government, a challenge inviting Liberty to defend itself in battle. I enlisted for the war. I am well aware that among disinterested patriots the matter of rank is not worthy of consideration, yet I frankly confess that I would rather be a captain patriot, than a corporal patriot. I confidentially admit that I would rather get a hundred dollars a month than thirteen dollars, and I would rather command than be commanded.[12]

Trumbull personally traveled to Des Moines to meet with Governor Kirkwood, who had called a special war session of the Iowa Legislature. Trumbull offered the services of his Butler County Union Guards and Kirkwood accepted. Trumbull was one of dozens of such hometown officers the Governor received. Kirkwood would have his regiment.

The ten companies of volunteers that made up the First Iowa Volunteer Infantry were mustered into three-month enlistments on 14 May 1861 at the large military camp in Keokuk, Iowa. This camp served as the jumping off point for Iowa soldiers heading south. Trumbull and his Butler County Union Guards were not included in the first regiment, but the Governor's proclamation made clear that they would be needed:

> If more companies are formed and reported, than can be received under the present call, their services will be required in the event of another requisition upon the state.[13]

Trumbull and his men did not have to wait long. At the end of May, Kirkwood ordered the rest of the militia companies to be brought up to full strength and stand ready to be mustered, this time for three-year enlistments.

Governor Kirkwood ordered the companies to assemble at the military encampment at Keokuk in the first two weeks of June. To get the volunteers to the designated rendezvous point, the Governor ordered that the railroads provide transportation. The Dubuque and Sioux City Railroad had been built east to the Cedar Valley by the spring of 1861 with Cedar Falls as the end of track. Train schedules were recalculated and it was announced that a locomotive and cars would be ready to roll from Cedar Falls on the fourth day of June. The train would take the valley volunteers east to Dubuque. From there they would be transported by steamship to Keokuk.[14]

The last week of May was exciting, frantic, tragic, and wondrously romantic. The farm towns of the Cedar Valley were ablaze with excitement. Hometown bands played martial music for rally after rally; old veterans of the War of 1812 and the Mexican War marched in parades and cheered the old flag. Politicians on every level of government stepped up to speaker's podiums to make their patriotic positions clear, and the militia captains took their turns as speakers, promising to bring victory and glory. Women gathered in great sewing bees to make pants, shirts, socks, caps, and the underclothes necessary for the great adventure. Mothers cried for their departing sons; fathers, too, shed prideful tears.

In Clarksville, early morning, Monday, 3 June 1861, a final rally was held for Trumbull and his Butler County Union Guards on the town square. More patriotic speeches were made and tear-filled eyes were evident as the men prepared to leave town. The departure was a spectacle: a full wagon train of friends and relatives escorted the soldiers.

This was the second time Trumbull had left Christiana to go to war, and this time she had three sons, ten and younger. She was also pregnant again and would be left to manage on her own. There were many such wives in Iowa. (The new Trumbull baby was another son, Ellsworth, named in honor of Colonel Ephraim E. Ellsworth of New York, a Union volunteer and first martyr to the Union. Many Northern sons were named for him.)[15]

It seemed as if all of the Upper Cedar Valley was on the move that morning. Every town had sons in one or another captain's company, and they were all heading for the railhead in Cedar Falls. Waverly, in Bremer County, sent a wagon train of forty teams and over three hundred citizens to escort twenty volunteers.[16]

As Trumbull's column made its way down the valley, farm boys who had joined his company left their chores, said goodbye to their parents, and took their places in the column. By the time Trumbull reached the Black Hawk County line, he had over eighty men in his ranks. He planned to march some six miles east of Cedar Falls to Waterloo, the Black Hawk County seat, where the last twenty-seven recruits for the Union Guards were waiting.

As Cedar Falls was the railhead, this was one of the most important days in the town's history and the people had done it up with pride. It was as if the state fair and the Fourth of July had merged into one. Thousands of people were in town. Flags hung in nearly every window; a large banner was draped across Main Street, and many more flags waved in the summer breeze from poles in lawns and on the city square in Overman Park. Hundreds of wagons lined the banks of the Cedar River where a huge ongoing picnic was in progress. The town had two old War of 1812 cannons which were fired at regular intervals, their booming heard by the farmers for miles around.

Every time a new wagon train arrived escorting volunteers, the people of Cedar Falls welcomed them with full honors. The pride of Cedar Falls was its new company, the Pioneer Greys, commanded by Captain John Smith, the owner of the Carter House Hotel. The town's tailors and over sixty women had held a long sewing session during the week and each of the Pioneer Greys was dressed in matching gray wool trousers, navy blue cotton shirts, and gray caps. The Waverly wagon train arrived about noon, and Trumbull's train reached town at 3:00 in the afternoon. As Trumbull's column got close to town, they were met and escorted to Overman Park by the Cedar Falls brass band playing from the back of a brightly painted wagon drawn by four horses and escorted to Overman Park. Captain Smith had his Pioneer Greys drawn up in military formation, waiting to meet the Butler County Union Guards. Trumbull formed his men into formation and exchanged salutes and cheers with the Pioneer Greys.[17]

It was a pleasant day in Cedar Falls. The people offered food and ice water, and there was still plenty of space to camp beneath the cedar trees that lined and shaded the banks of the river. It was tempting for the Union Guards to remain there and meet the morning train with the Pioneer Greys, but that would be an insult to the Waterloo members of the Union Guards. Trumbull allowed his men, their families, and friends to rest for less than an hour. Then, with the Cedar Falls Pioneer Greys acting as their escort out of town, he led his wagon train to Waterloo.

It was evening as they neared the outskirts of Waterloo. As they got closer, fifty mounted men appeared on the road. They were Waterloo's newly formed cavalry company, accompanied by the Waterloo brass band in its own wagon. Trumbull called his men into marching order, and, escorted by the cavalry and the brass band, they proudly marched down Commercial Street past hundreds of enthusiastic citizens to the Sherman House Hotel where a stage held the mayor, a local minister, and other leading citizens. The horsemen and Trumbull's infantry stopped in front of the stage and faced the dignitaries. The band played martial music and over two thousand people cheered. Waterloo had its own cannon that was fired again and again in salute.

Trumbull took his place on the stage, thanked Waterloo for its kind reception, and led his men in a loud cheer for its citizens. He then let his men break ranks and mingle for a while. Later that evening, Trumbull and his Butler County people joined with the Waterloo folks for a nighttime rally on Waterloo's courthouse square. The *Waterloo Courier* reported that:

> The gathering was large and enthusiastic. Elder Eberhart, W. M. Newton and Captain Trumbull were the speakers. Their efforts were timely and appropriate, and breathed a spirit of patriotism and loyalty to the Union, which does honor to themselves and justice to that government which has held its protecting arm over them as they have grown and prospered.[18]

Trumbull and the Butler County train made camp along the Cedar River. He and his volunteers were prepared to leave the Cedar Valley in the morning. The Dubuque and Sioux City Railroad sent a locomotive and five passenger cars to Cedar Falls in the early morning hours. The train was turned around in the roundhouse and moved to the Cedar Falls depot, facing east towards Waterloo and Dubuque. Cedar Falls patriots decorated the train with flags and bunting and, after a morning's celebration, put their Pioneer Greys on board. Along with the men were a brass band and dozens of friends; even the baggage car was filled.

The crowded train arrived in Waterloo at 10:12, and the Cedar Falls passengers poured out to greet the thousands of friends there. The two brass bands tried to outdo each other and played one military tune after another. The Waterloo cannon was fired, and Waterloo's cavalry company escorted the Butler County Union Guards from their camp to the depot. The Pioneer Greys stood proudly in their new uniforms and cheered Trumbull and his men. More speeches were made, more tears were shed, and Trumbull had difficulty getting his men on board as they each tried to say farewell to a loved one a final time. Finally, the Greys, the Guards, over a hundred of their friends, and the Cedar Falls band all managed to get on board. The conductor got the doors closed and gave the engineer the signal to advance. In a very dramatic fashion, the engineer slowly backed the train up, building steam, and then blasted forward as fast as possible, passing the depot at full throttle. The people cheered, the cannon boomed, and ladies waved their kerchiefs and cried. The *Waterloo Courier* said this:

> And thus, Waterloo has laid her first votive offering upon the shrine of our common country. Her numbers are not many, but true and brave, and generous are they who leave a home of comfort and plenty to undergo the fatigues and dangers of a soldier's life....[19]

The train traveled slowly toward Dubuque. Every town along the way had its own celebration, its own brass band, and its own citizens who wanted to salute the volunteers. Each stop was a reason for Trumbull, Smith, and others to make more speeches. The train reached its destination at 4:00. A reporter for the *Dubuque Daily Times* said this about Trumbull's company: "This company is 108 men strong and composed of some regular giants. One man is 6 feet 4 inches in height, eight more are six feet tall."[20]

Dubuque was Dennis Mahoney country—a town with some of the state's most outspoken opponents of Mr. Lincoln's war. Mahoney's *Dubuque Herald* was an important dissonant voice. But the city was also filled with pro-Union patriots and they were out in full force that day. The Dubuque Washington Guards, another volunteer militia company called into service, met the Cedar Valley volunteers with full military pomp and ceremony. A German marching band escorted the Pioneer Greys and Union Guards to a city park for another celebration and more speeches. Lieutenant Fitzroy Sessions of the Pioneer Greys took the speaker's stage and denounced Mahoney and his newspaper. Sessions called on the good people of Dubuque to watch the traitors at home while he and his men were away at war.[21]

After the celebration the men were marched through town with the German band playing and the people of Dubuque crowding the street. That evening, after their long day, the men were escorted to their quarters. The Greys were housed in a large brick building by the Mississippi River while Trumbull's Union Guards stayed in the city hall.[22]

The next day the two Cedar Valley companies, now joined by the Dubuque company, boarded the steamboat *Key City*. The dock was crowded with well-wishing citizens, many who were friends or relatives of the volunteers. But not all on the dock were cheering. Some openly shouted insults at the recruits and their abolitionist president. When someone threw a rock at the boys on the boat, Lieutenant Sessions grabbed his Bowie knife, stuck it between his teeth, drew his brand new revolver (presented to him the night before in Cedar Falls), and jumped from the steamboat deck. He landed on both feet and punched the man he thought was the rock-thrower, knocking him down. He then turned on the others in deadly fury, but the boat was leaving the dock. Sessions turned, ran, and managed to leap across a few feet of water onto the deck of the moving boat. The men cheered Sessions, and the *Cedar Falls Gazette* reported the incident as "first blood for the Pioneer Greys."[23]

The steamboat took the volunteers to Keokuk where they were assigned quarters. A few days later ten companies from across the state were drawn up in military formation to be sworn into service in the Third Iowa Volunteer Infantry. The Butler County Union Guards became Company I and the Pioneer Greys became Company K. Lieutenant S. D. Thompson, author of *Recollections With the Third Iowa Regiment,* the single best history of the first three years of the regiment, described that moment:

> We were mustered into the service of the United States by Lieut. Alexander Chambers, of the regular army, since colonel of the 16th Iowa. Before this ceremony took place, the Articles of War were read to us, and from them we inferred that it was no easy matter to be a good soldier, and not at all safe to be a poor one. Those who did not wish to be sworn in after hearing them read, were allowed to decline. A few did so; and the farewell salutations these "deserters" as we chose to call them, received from their late comrades were not at all calculated to make them feel joyful or proud. [24]

About two weeks later Editor William Haddock of the *Butler County Jeffersonian* visited the Butler County Union Guards at their Keokuk camp and wrote:

> The company was in good health…they have been complimented on their soldierly appearance and general good conduct. Captain T. sends his best regards to all inquiring friends, and says that although the organizing of his Company has cost him much labor and money, he has given it freely, and if his life shall be necessary in this struggle, it will be given just as freely, in the belief that a generous American people will not suffer his family to go uncared for. If this is the way an adopted citizen feels, who was born upon English soil, what ought to be the impulses of those who have never been fed by any but American mothers.[25]

CHAPTER 5

The Matter of Rank

A Civil War regiment was made up of ten one-hundred-man companies, lettered "A" through "K" (with "J" omitted). A captain commanded each company while a colonel, lieutenant colonel, and major commanded each regiment. Trumbull and the other captains had raised their companies without guarantees of their eventual regimental designations. However, because the men elected each company's officers and noncommissioned officers, it was understood that those ranks would continue. In turn, the captains and lieutenants believed that when they were assigned to a new regiment, they would elect its commanding officers. But they also understood that such elections would be subject to the approval of Governor Kirkwood, who, by law, appointed all field and medical officers.[1]

Trumbull and the rest of the captains knew that they were playing for high stakes. There was no limit to the political advancement of a successful officer, and successful officers would have long coattails. Politics aside, career advancement in any field was enhanced by a good war record and high army rank. Trumbull, a lawyer, would carry the prestige of his army title into every courtroom in which he tried a case. Professional coattails were as important as those in politics. The Third Iowa Infantry contained some very ambitious captains. Each believed he was fit for any office in the regiment, and the men of their companies were fiercely supportive of their favorites.

The captains also understood negative coattails. Service with an inferior officer could, at the worst, get them killed along with their volunteers. Association with a poor officer could ruin their chances of individual recognition and advancement. Rank, politics, and war mixed together in a witch's brew of internal discord that all but ruined many Civil War soldiers and regiments.

When the men of the ten Third Iowa Infantry companies were mustered into the army at Camp Ellsworth in Keokuk, the Governor had not yet appointed the regiments' field officers. The captains chose to recognize an unofficial seniority system that put Captain Richard Herron in command.

Herron, thirty years old, was born in Pennsylvania but had been raised and educated in Kentucky where he and his elder brother, Francis, attended military school. In the 1850s the brothers moved to Dubuque where they established the Herron Brothers Bank. In Dubuque they also helped organize Iowa's first militia company, the Governor's Greys. When the war came each brother organized a militia company and was elected captain. Francis Herron and his company were included in Kirkwood's first call as part of the First Iowa Infantry. Herron was recognized for gallantry at the Battle of Wilson's Creek, Missouri (10 Aug. 1861) and was later made lieutenant colonel of William Vandever's Ninth Iowa Infantry. By the war's end Francis Herron was one of Iowa's three major generals.[2]

Richard Herron, with his military school education and experience in the Governor's Greys, was the best qualified to begin training the new recruits, but military discipline was a hard thing for citizen soldiers. Lieutenant S. D. Thomson, in his *Recollections With the Third Iowa Regiment* said of Richard Herron:

> He was in every respect a gentleman; but his discipline, though wholesome and correct, was such as our democratic ideas enabled us poorly to appreciate.[3]

Herron and the other captains knew that his command would be temporary. Governor Kirkwood had already made his choice for commanding officer—Nelson G. Williams of Dyersville. Yet few in the regiment had any idea who Williams was. Lieutenant Thompson said this about him:

> It was said that he was a military man, and yet a private citizen, and not a politician. Many had spoken in favor of him; no one against him. He was the man.[4]

Nelson G. Williams was born in New York in 1823. As a young man he did very well in business, and in 1855 he moved to a farm between Dyersville and Dubuque, Iowa, where he became connected with some of the most powerful men in the state. He had been a cadet at West Point for almost three years and a classmate of U. S. Grant. But, due to poor grades and a lack of funds, he did not graduate or receive a commission. He had also been a member of a militia company in New York.[5] When Governor Kirkwood made his proclamation, Williams began calling himself Major Williams and started gathering as much support as possible for a claim to regimental command. When he approached Governor Kirkwood, he had some very powerful backers.

Both the *Dubuque Weekly Times* and the *Dubuque Daily Times* threw their support

Samuel Jordan Kirkwood
(*Drawing by Ron Prahl*)

behind Williams. Another important friend was Henry L. Stout, the most successful lumberman in Iowa. Stout was a millionaire and a man who was heard in the state's highest political circles. In May 1861 Stout wrote to Governor Kirkwood saying that he believed Williams ". . . to be preeminently qualified for the position."[6]

The most influential of Williams's backers was William Boyd Allison of Dubuque. Allison was a close friend of Henry Stout, but more importantly, he was one of the chief political organizers of Kirkwood's 1860 election as governor. Leland L. Sage, Allison's biographer, said this about the relationship between Allison and Kirkwood:

> Undoubtedly the victorious Kirkwood was not only grateful to Allison but po-
> litically obligated to him as well. This is one of the truly important personal and
> political associations in Allison's life.[7]

When war came Allison was appointed "special aide" to Governor Kirkwood; his duties included seeing to the needs of the new regiments. From military posts to railroad passes, from guns and blankets to medical supplies and horse shoes, William Boyd Allison was the most important bureaucrat in the state. Allison wrote to Kirkwood on Williams's behalf in May saying of Williams:

> …he is a good citizen and worthy officer, if you can give him some position in one
> of the two regiments now forming, I am well satisfied he will discharge the duties
> with credit to himself & honor to the state.[8]

Williams, confident of success, traveled to Keokuk in June to convince the elected officers of the Third Iowa Infantry to hurry the process of getting the regiment's field officers selected and commissioned.

On 17 June 1861 twenty-one officers of the regiment held a meeting in the parlor of the Dunning House Hotel in Keokuk. Their purpose was to elect their field officers. Captain William Milo Stone of "B" Company from Knoxville was named "President of the meeting."[9]

Stone was born in New York in 1827, came to Iowa in 1854 as a lawyer, and later, became editor of the Republican newspaper, the *Knoxville Journal*. Stone was a founder of Iowa's Republican Party, a delegate to its first convention, and one of its presidential electors in the 1856 election. In 1857 he was elected judge of the 11th District. When the war came he resigned his seat as judge and went to work recruiting men. He was a very religious man, a moral man, and his men called him their "Presbyterian captain."[10]

The first thing the officers did was recommend, by acclamation, that Nelson Williams be appointed as colonel of the regiment "without delay."

The next thing was to elect the field officers. Richard Herron was elected lieutenant colonel with fourteen out of sixteen votes, with the other officers not voting.

The next vote was for major. William Stone and Matthew Trumbull were the most popular choices. In the first ballot Stone received seven votes and Trumbull five, with the rest divided among other candidates. With neither Stone nor Trumbull having a clear majority, another vote was held between those two officers. In the second ballot Trumbull received eleven votes and Stone got ten.

Lieutenant Sessions of Cedar Falls then recommended that a committee be formed to present a transcript of the proceedings to Governor Kirkwood.[11]

Nelson Williams agreed to take the results directly to Governor Kirkwood and left the Keokuk camp immediately, saying that he would be back as quickly as possible with the official commissions signed by the Governor.

Two days later, five officers, including Captain Smith and Lieutenant Sessions of the Pioneer Greys who had not initially voted for Trumbull, sent an independent letter to the governor saying that they:

> …desire to concur in the action of the majority of those who voted to recommend Captain M. M. Trumbull for the position of major of the 3rd Regiment. We recommend Captain Trumbull as an officer of experience, and believe him fully competent to perform the duties of Major.
>
> Not having voted in the majority is the reason why we desire to present the governor with this additional testimonial.[12]

Not every officer concurred with the vote. Captain John Scott of "E" Company, from Nevada, was not present at the Keokuk meeting and he had many objections.

Scott was one of the most colorful and intensely ambitious captains in the regiment. Born in Ohio in 1824, he traveled widely as a young man. In 1846 when the Mexican War broke out, Scott enlisted in a regiment of Kentucky volunteers along with the famous abolitionist editor and politician Cassius M. Clay. Scott, Clay, and seventy others were captured and held captive in Mexico City for eight months. Scott moved to Iowa in 1856 and in 1859 he was elected to the State Senate from Story County. He also served in Kirkwood's special war session, but finally resigned to raise a company of volunteers.[13]

Scott, a political ally and friend of Kirkwood, took it upon himself to evaluate the results of the election and comment to the Governor.

> My Dear Governor,
>
> I returned from a short visit home last evening and have been a great deal mortified to learn some things connected with the 3d Regt. that occurred during my absence. They only serve to show the immense importance of getting a first class man to lead us. Let me urge you not to act until you are satisfied-and yet to delay in organization is felt as a great annoyance by all of us. But far better a month's delay under our present inefficients, than a permanent organization that would ruin us.

From what I can hear of Capt. Herron since I came down I am led to believe he is not likely to be so efficient as I hoped to find him. It is a delicate matter for me to make this suggestion, but you will understand the spirit that prompts it. Personally I have a high regard for him.

I send you the following extract from a letter written by an esteemed friend at Dubuque…

"How under heaven that man Nels Williams could secure such a position is a mystery to me. The idea of his claiming to be a West Point Graduate! He was there, when a youth, less than a year, and was then *expelled* for insubordination, as I learned from credible authority. Dubuque has been sufficiently disgraced."[14]

While Governor Kirkwood delayed in making the field appointments, on 27 June 1861, less than three weeks after being mustered, the Third Iowa was shipped south to Missouri. The state of Iowa issued the men their first official uniforms, old state dragoon uniforms of heavy wool colored gray. The men were also issued their first weapons, 1848 smoothbore Springfield muskets, the last smoothbore musket to be issued to U.S. troops. They were given a few rounds of ammunition, but they had to carry them in their pockets because cartridge boxes, canteens, and other accouterments had not arrived. Not very military, but by 1861 standards they were considered ready for combat.[15]

Williams had not returned with the commissions when the regiment was shipped out, so Richard Herron remained in command during the transfer to Missouri, but there was no real officer above the rank of captain.

While the regiment was encamped at Utica, Missouri, engaged in guarding railroads, word came that Colonel Williams was due to arrive any day and was bringing the expected commissions with him. The message listed the names of the new officers.

To the surprise, and offense, of Matthew Trumbull and his fellow captains, Governor Kirkwood had chosen to ignore the Keokuk vote and kept his own counsel concerning the appointments. John Scott was promoted to lieutenant colonel, rather than Richard Herron, and William M. Stone, not Matthew Trumbull, was promoted to major. As soon as the news arrived, Richard Herron stepped down and Scott took command of the regiment.[16]

Everyone anxiously waited for Williams's arrival. Lieutenant S. D. Thompson explained the concern:

While we were camped at Utica, Col. Williams arrived and assumed command. Of course all watched his conduct with great scrutiny. He was the man who, more than any other, held in his hand our destiny. His proper care would give us supplies, health, discipline, and, in every way, promote our efficiency, good appearance and good name. His conduct in battle would greatly influence the chances of victory and glory on the one hand, and of defeat and disgrace on the other.[17]

CHAPTER 6

The Shelbina Affair

Colonel Williams was faced with a tremendous challenge. To lead rather than command was the critical skill necessary for Civil War officers. They were in charge of citizen soldiers, men who had willingly left their homes and families, men who demanded respect. Any officer not capable of inspiring men to battle—while at the same time mollifying a thousand wounded egos, pleasing voters, and fending off jealous, ambitious, junior officers—had little future in a Civil War army.

The gray-haired Williams was a powerful man with dark angry eyes—an impatient man with a violent temper. (He once punched out a Dubuque tough when the fellow struck his horse.) Even Williams's most ardent supporters agreed that he was not a tactful man, but he seemed to know the business of soldiering. When Williams took command at Utica, Missouri, he knew that his regiment was deep inside enemy territory, ill-equipped, and poorly trained. Yet he was determined to bring it into shape as quickly as possible.

The first thing the new colonel did was to establish, and strictly enforce, military discipline in his camp. He tried to keep the good will of the people of Missouri by making sure that no soldier was allowed out of camp without permission. No stories were told of his men leaving camp to get drunk in town or of them harassing local citizens. Lieutenant Thompson said this:

> …under Williams, it was a serious thing to disobey orders; and breaking guard was a risk which very few were willing to run. Whatever may be said against the colonel, the discipline we attained under him…was highly creditable to him. It was in consequence of this discipline that our regiment had a good name among the citizens of Missouri, such as volunteer troops seldom gain among strangers or enemies.[1]

Captain Trumbull concurred with Thompson. In a letter to William Haddock of the *Butler County Jeffersonian*, Trumbull wrote:

> The boys of Company "I" have made themselves very popular with the citizens about here, by their gentlemanly conduct, and uniform good behavior. They are well treated by them and highly respected, and the same thing may be said of the whole 3d Regiment.[2]

Nelson G. Williams
(*Drawing by Ron Prahl*)

Williams's strict camp discipline was coupled with an almost fanatic emphasis on drill. Civil War drill was difficult to learn; a company of one hundred men had to learn to act as one. The men had to learn to load and fire their muzzle-loading weapons with uniform precision. They had to learn how to march by column, turn the column to oblique or flank positions, and switch from column to battle line quickly, under fire, to the sound of a military drum. Companies had to learn to maneuver as parts of regiments, regiments as parts of brigades, and brigades had to work as parts of divisions. Each officer and each soldier in the ranks had to know his part. There was no substitute for drill; it was the center of a soldier's life. Nothing separated the veteran from the rookie like proficiency in drill.

But drill was hard work, especially in the Missouri heat, with troops dressed in heavy wool winter dragoon uniforms. Plus, Williams showed no patience with subordinates. He often cursed the troops during drill and insulted officers in front of their men. Lieutenant Thompson wrote:

> His efforts to preserve good discipline were certainly commendable; but his decisions were rash and hasty. His temper was quick and ungovernable, and his judgment part of the time under the control of his temper. The least mistake of a soldier was sufficient to put him into a violent fit of rage. Of course such manifestations tended to create a feeling of hatred and contempt toward him on the part of his men; and so frequently did these occur that they soon came to despise at once his rank and authority.[3]

Drill and discipline may have caused problems for Colonel Williams, but poor opinions of Civil War officers could be changed with victory. A despised disciplinarian was generally forgiven for harshness on the parade ground if his performance in battle was impressive. Yet, Colonel Williams's greatest misfortune was that again and again he seemed to be denied the opportunity to take on the enemy in a stand up fight and salvage his reputation.

Missouri was a unique state during the Civil War—a border state that both sides claimed. Union victories at the battles of Wilson's Creek, Missouri, and Pea Ridge, Arkansas, had kept Missouri in the Union, but the Confederacy wanted it back. Missouri rebels fought for a Confederate Missouri as regular Confederate forces, but also as guerrilla fighters, mounted outlaws who carried on a backwoods sort of blood feud with Unionists. Union soldiers sent to Missouri also played many roles at once. They were invading Yankees, an army of occupation hated by Missouri Confederates, and they were also allies of loyal Missouri Unionists. Duty in Missouri would have been difficult for the most experienced troops; it was next to impossible for new recruits. Matthew Trumbull, in his first letter from the front to Editor William Haddock of the *Butler County Jeffersonian,* expressed the difficulties of serving in Missouri:

> Friend Haddock—
> We have had a pretty hard time of it since we have been in Missouri, but we would not care a pin for that, if we could only get a fair fight out of the secessionists; but there is not much chance of that. Their game is assassination and arson. Whenever they can lie in wait, fire and run away, they adopt that mode of warfare.[4]

Trumbull also expressed his anger at Governor Kirkwood for ignoring the officers' election in Keokuk:

> We left Keokuk two weeks ago yesterday, about a thousand men strong. We went on a couple of ferry boats fastened together. The men had to stand on the deck in the pouring rain all the way from Keokuk to Hannibal. We staid at Hannibal on Sunday, and on Monday we went out in the cars for Utica, about 135 miles, which place we reached about midnight. The men laid down and slept on the ground that night, hungry and tired, and the next morning we pitched our tents and called it Camp Herron in honor of Captain Herron who up to this time had command of our regiment, the Governor of Iowa having with inexcusable neglect delayed the appointment of our regimental officers, and when he did appoint them, he gave commissions in defiance of the expressed wishes of the officers of the regiment.[5]

Colonel Williams's Missouri command extended over many miles. In the course of the summer he had his headquarters at Utica, Chillicothe, Brookfield, and Macon City, but his companies were stationed at different points along the Hannibal and St. Joseph Railroad, parceled out to guard bridges, chase guerrillas, and police towns.

The principle Confederate force in that part of Missouri was under Thomas Harris, a former congressman from Missouri who commanded a large force of mounted infantry. On 5 July 1861, Colonel Williams, in cooperation with the colonel of the Sixteenth Illinois Infantry that was brigaded with the Third Iowa, devised a plan to encircle Harris at the town of Monroe Station. Four companies of the Third Iowa were assigned to the expedition. Colonel Williams kept the campaign a secret until the last minute, so it was not until the men had their Sunday morning breakfast that Williams gave the order for the designated companies to pack and board the train. Williams hurried the men and shouted at them for taking too long. Many men had

to leave their belongings behind and never saw them again. The four companies got on the train and by late afternoon had reached Palmyra where they joined two companies of the Sixteenth Illinois and one company of Missouri Unionists—the Hannibal Home Guards, who had a six-pound cannon. The combined force boarded another train and traveled eighteen miles to Monroe Station where they got off the cars and formed into a battalion column of about four hundred and fifty men.

Colonel Williams gave command of the battalion to Captain Herron, but, in a move designed to insult Lieutenant Colonel John Scott, his principal foe in the regiment, Williams allowed Scott to go along, but merely as an observer. Lieutenant S. D. Thompson wrote, "The enlisted men did not, at the time, understand this shameful trick, but wondered to see Capt. Herron giving orders to the battalion in the presence of Lt. Col. Scott."[6]

The battalion march was a mess from the beginning. It rained hard all night and, when the men could not make their way over the muddy roads, the march was halted. The Third Iowa companies' ammunition got wet because the men had to carry it in their jacket pockets. The men were forced to take shelter for the night in some abandoned buildings. Although the next morning was bright and sunny, the original plan had been to make a night march and surprise the enemy at dawn. The storm had changed all that. Harris and his rebels certainly knew that Herron's battalion was on its way and they would be prepared. The Union battalion was up against an enemy force believed to be nearly a thousand strong with at least three field pieces. Outnumbered or not, Herron decided to attack.

The afternoon was a confusion of marches, chases, and a brief skirmish near a place called Hagar's Woods, but the enemy force could not be found. Herron finally gave up and countermarched the battalion back to Monroe Station. The retreating column was shot at a few times as it marched, but no one was hit. The men approached their old camp about eleven o'clock that night and found the dark sky lit by the railroad depot. The train they had left behind that morning was in full flames, torched by the enemy. The men of the battalion marched to the burning station, fearing attack at any moment. Captain Herron received reports that the surrounding woods were filled with rebels; Harris and his Confederates were no longer the hunted, they were the hunters. The Union troops put out the fire, dug trenches, checked their ammunition, and settled in for a siege hoping that Colonel Williams would come to their rescue.

Matthew Trumbull and his company were not in Herron's battalion; they had remained in Utica with Colonel Williams. In his letter to William Haddock, Trumbull described his company's part in the rescue of Herron and his battalion:

> On Wednesday night we heard that the secessionists had burned some railroad bridges, torn up the track and destroyed some depots and trains, and that our boys were surrounded by about 2000 of the enemy, and needed help. Four companies —mine among the number—immediately started under command of Col. Williams for the scene of action, some miles distant. The men were packed together in freight cars, but not a grumble or murmur was heard. We had a great many delays on the road, and it was not until the next evening that we reached the burning bridge, which stopped our further progress. All this time, about 30 hours, our men had nothing to eat. All along the road we heard all sorts of rumors about our boys—that they were defeated, that they were surrounded, etc. When we got to the bridge we heard that they still held their own. Here we had to leave the cars, ford the river, and take it on foot. We were yet about eleven miles from the scene of the battle. Here some bread was procured and when it was about to be distributed, the men called out, "Never mind the bread, we want to assist our comrades," and we went through the burning ruins of the bridge, and over the torn track. It was near midnight when we reached Monroe, the scene of the conflict; but to our mortification and disappointment, the battle was over, the enemy had been beaten off, and scattered.[7]

There had not really been a battle at Monroe Station. The Confederates retreated when they spotted Williams and his reinforcements. The men of the besieged battalion cheered their rescuers, but Lieutenant Thompson wrote: "They complained loudly of Col. Williams for tardiness and hesitancy."[8]

Williams took part of his command back to Utica, but Trumbull and his men remained in Monroe Station for a few days. They found a deserted house with a full larder and lived very well. When the owner of the house returned, he asked that he be allowed to salvage his furniture. Trumbull allowed him to do so on the condition that the man should swear allegiance to the Union and the Constitution, which he did. Trumbull was very proud that his men did not loot the house and only took the "eatables…which their famished conditioned justified."[9]

Trumbull's company took the train to Macon City where Colonel Williams had duty for them. It was at this place that Trumbull wrote his letter to Editor Haddock:

> We staid on the cars all night at Macon City. About two miles west of that place, there is a railroad bridge across the East fork of the Chariton River. About day break we got there, the cars stopped, and the order passed along for Company I. Company I formed in two minutes. A little dose of provisions was put out. The orders were short—"Guard that bridge,"—and on went the train. We stacked our arms, took our breakfast, coffee, taters, and bacon, no bread. After breakfast we took a smoke, told a few yarns, and then I gave orders to build a fort; and although the boys were very tired, and almost exhausted with their labors and want of rest, they went to work with a will, and in a few hours they had it done. They named it Fort Trumbull, gave three cheers and went to supper. Our position is a strong one. No thousand men in Missouri can either take or burn the bridge. The Colonel promised to send us provisions as soon as he could get back to camp. He will not be able to do it, for some bridges west of us were burned last night, and we are cut off from communications both east and west. Our provisions are short. Today I shall send the boys out a hunting deer. They are poor marksmen, for when they fire at a deer they generally bring down a fat ox. Of course, after the accident has happened, it would be a pity to waste the critter, so we generally eat him.[10]

Rumors about Colonel Williams spread rapidly. It was said that he had been drunk and gotten lost on the way to Monroe Station and that he was a coward and deliberately delayed the rescue. How many, if any, of the stories were true has been lost in the charges and defenses concerning the colonel. Still, the rumors did much to destroy his reputation and give ammunition to his enemies.

On 12 August 1861, with John Scott leading, most of the officers in the regiment signed a petition and presented it to the brigade commander, General Stephen A. Hurlbut, preferring court martial charges against Williams. They charged Williams with a series of offenses including: neglecting to provide for his soldiers, drunkenness, cowardice, and conduct unbecoming an officer and a gentleman. The charges told of

Williams threatening and insulting his officers in public and in front of their men. They said that he had carried a canteen of liquor around his neck on the trip to and from Monroe Station and became so drunk and angry that he drew his pistol and threatened to shoot an officer of the 16th Illinois.

Matthew Trumbull was one of the officers who signed the petition, but he was also the only one who placed the qualifier "As far as knowledge extends" next to his signature. The names of Captain Smith and Lieutenant Sessions of Cedar Falls did not appear on the petition. The Cedar Falls officers and most of the Pioneer Greys supported Williams (who had promoted Sessions to the rank of adjutant).[11]

Historian Larry J. Daniel described General Hurlbut as "...an Illinois Republican known for his embarrassing drunken binges and shady land deals."[12] Hurlbut had plenty of accusers of his own, and he chose to ignore the petition against Williams. The general's refusal to bring charges against Colonel Williams caused the regiment's surgeon, Dr. Thomas O. Edwards of Dubuque, to follow the petition with a personal letter to Governor Kirkwood asking him to intercede:

> We have commissions signed by you—we are citizens of Iowa—are volunteers "during the war," impelled by a determination to defend the Union, the Constitution and the upholding of the laws—we are not now in your state, yet we are of your state, our families, our possessions are there, we are the representatives of your state and we deserve protection for our lives—honor our feelings....
>
> We sincerely believe as gentlemen & soldiers every charge in that communication can be fully proved & moreover that so demoralized is the once boasted 3rd Reg. of Iowa that it would be unwise indeed unsafe to go into battle under its present colonel.[13]

Surgeon Edwards's attack on Williams was another example of the division in the regiment over Williams. Even the medical department was torn. Assistant Surgeon Dr. Daniel M. Cool of Waverly supported Williams and was no friend of Edwards. Contrary to Edwards's request, the governor chose not to interfere in a military matter. Williams was not charged, but the affair was far from finished.

In the first week of September, Colonel Williams commanded a battalion made up of companies from the Third Iowa and the Second Kansas Infantry. A company of Missouri Home Guard cavalry joined the infantry, giving Williams about seven hundred men. Williams was ordered to march from Kirksville to Shelbina by way of Paris, Missouri. Lieutenant S. D. Thompson wrote that the first night at Paris Williams and a Kansas officer got roaring drunk. Williams was so drunk that all the officers of the Third Iowa agreed to ignore his orders until he sobered up.[14]

Thompson said that Williams was sober in the morning and the battalion proceeded by train to Shelbina, with the Missouri cavalry riding close to the cars. When they arrived at Shelbina, they discovered that General Hurlbut and the rest of the

Union troops were gone. Even more serious were sightings of a large rebel army nearby. Williams's soldiers occupied the town and prepared to defend it against an enemy he believed to number in the thousands. By morning the enemy troops were clearly visible, marching by column along the valley beyond the town and then forming into battle line to the north of town. The rebel line was almost two miles long with two artillery pieces placed at different points. More troops could be seen waiting in reserve a half mile beyond the line itself.

The Confederate commander, Martin Green, sent a courier over under a flag of truce with an offer to accept the surrender of Williams and his men, giving Williams a half hour to decide. Williams received the messenger and told him to return with his answer, "Go to hell." When the Confederate courier left, Williams ordered the women and children out of town and wired Hurlbut asking for help. Hurlbut replied, telling Williams to hold out and reinforcements would be there before dark. All this time the enemy forces continued to maneuver to envelop the town and cut off any chance of retreat. The commanding officer of the Second Kansas with Williams's battalion said that he intended to get his men out of the trap before the rebels surrounded the place.[15]

Williams, not being able to convince the Kansas troops to stay, ignored Hurlbut's message and ordered a full retreat. He hurriedly got his men aboard the train, leaving behind several baggage wagons and much camp equipment. The train raced away from Shelbina, screened by the Missouri cavalry, as Confederate cannons fired at the cars. Many officers expected Williams to halt at the next town, Clarence, turn around, dig in, face the enemy, and wait for Hurlbut, but Williams kept the cars going. When Williams's train reached Macon City, he found General Hurlbut there on his way with two hundred and fifty reinforcements. Hurlbut was furious and strongly rebuked Williams and his officers. Hurlbut's scolding contributed to the officers' anger at their colonel.[16]

The military situation in Northern Missouri was in shambles. General John Charles Frémont, 1856 candidate for the presidency on the Republican Party ticket and now commanding officer of the District of Missouri, sent General John Pope to straighten it out. Pope gave the difficulties of the Third Iowa a top priority. The retreat from Shelbina, the rumors of drunkenness, and the written complaints from officers against both Hurlbut and Williams caused General Pope to order that charges be brought against the two officers. Both men were ordered to report to St. Louis where they were placed under house arrest. The charges against Hurlbut were quickly dropped, but Williams was charged with being drunk on duty, cowardice in the face of the enemy, and for, while in a drunken rage, threatening the life of a train conductor during the Shelbina retreat.[17]

Colonel Williams's enemies were enthusiastic over the news of his arrest. Lieutenant S. D. Thompson believed that Williams had been drunk on the Shelbina expedition and wrote that Williams committed a fault for which he "should have been dismissed from the service."[18]

Williams's friends rallied to his defense. A member of Cedar Falls's Pioneer Greys, writing under the pen name of Udonohu, wrote a long letter to the *Cedar Falls Gazette* in support of their colonel:

> To start with, I will simply say that anyone who says that Col. Williams has been incapacitated from duty through the effects of liquor lies. As to the other charges they amount to nothing, being wholly untrue.

The letter dismissed Surgeon Edwards by saying: "…the opinion of the regiment is that the excessive use of opium and other stimulants has driven him to an early dotage." The letter went on to say that those officers who made derogatory statements against Colonel Williams were merely, "aspirants for better positions than they now occupy." The letter demanded:

> …simple justice to a deeply injured man, one who in bravery, integrity, and all the attributes of a gentleman, a faithful and gallant officer, is as much above those who speak against him, as heaven is above hell.[19]

Williams's arrest meant that the Third Iowa Infantry would go into its first major battle under the command of Lieutenant Colonel John Scott.

CHAPTER 7

The Battle of Blue Mills Landing

Blue Mills Landing, less than five miles south of Liberty, Missouri, provided ferry service across the Missouri River to Kansas. Confederate forces retreating from Missouri needed to cross at Blue Mills. On 15 September 1861, Lieutenant Colonel John Scott received orders to take the Third Iowa from its camp at Macon City to Liberty. There he would meet a column of the Sixteenth Illinois Infantry under Colonel Smith and another from the Thirty-ninth Ohio Infantry. Once combined, they would march to the landing and intercept a large enemy force before it could cross the river into Kansas.

The Iowa men were anxious for a fight. Williams's retreat from Shelbina and his later arrest had disgraced the entire regiment; this was their chance to redeem the honor of the Third Iowa Infantry. Matthew Trumbull, in a letter to the *Dubuque Weekly Times,* explained:

John Scott
(*Drawing by Ron Prahl*)

...the Iowa boys were determined to show their friends at home, that they could fight, and would fight, and wipe out the undeserved reproach cast upon us by the Shelbina affair....[1]

John Scott had worked hard to undermine the authority of Colonel Williams, but, at the same time, he worked hard to earn the respect and confidence of the men. Where Williams was harsh, Scott was cordial and sympathetic. He presented himself as a friend to the men in the ranks, and it worked. Most in the regiment had confidence in him as they took to the field on the Blue Mills campaign. (However, the Pioneer Greys and some others would never forgive Scott for what he had done to Williams.)

The first thing the new commander did

was cull the regiment of any men who were too sick or weak to endure the campaign. This left Scott with a force of about five hundred men. He put his men aboard train cars at Macon City and they rode to Cameron, north of Liberty. Scott then took his men off the cars and prepared them to march to Liberty. Cameron citizens informed Scott that Confederate forces had passed through the town a few days before and had pillaged some warehouses. They told him that he might recognize the rebels because they had taken a supply of bright red shirts from one of the warehouses. (Scott's men were still wearing their heavy gray Iowa dragoon uniforms.)

Scott requisitioned several wagons and mule teams, loaded the regiment's baggage, and formed the men in a marching column with Matthew Trumbull and his Butler County Union Guards first in line. While preparing his wagons, the first of the promised reinforcements joined Scott. They included a seventy-man company of mounted Missouri Home Guards and a fourteen-man Missouri artillery battery with a six-pounder field piece. After inspecting the wagons, and the arms and accoutrements of the men, Scott mounted his little roan horse and gave the signal to march. Trumbull described the first day's march:

> We left Cameron about 3 o'clock in the afternoon of Sunday, the 15th. It was raining heavily and the roads were very muddy, with that slimy mud peculiar to Missouri. We marched about ten miles that evening, and then laid down upon the damp cold ground to rest, having but a little hay to sleep on, no tents....Notwithstanding all these privations and discomforts, the men were cheerful, laughing and joking, singing, smoking their pipes, and telling stories, and above all, firmly devoted to their duty.[2]

Scott had the men up early the next morning. He sent a few of the Missouri cavalrymen ahead as scouts. For the infantry, this day's march was pleasant. The rain had stopped and the roads were not as muddy as they had been, but wet enough to keep the dust down. The sun shone through the leaves of the trees that lined the roads, but it was not too hot and a breeze cooled the air. The little towns and farms along the way were deserted and the men fed well on the contents of the pantries and cellars they found.

Scott's column arrived in Centerville, about ten miles from Liberty, at sunset and Scott let the men make camp for the night. But Scott did not sleep—each moment he became more nervous. His Missouri scouts had brought news that Confederate troops were already marching through the streets of Liberty and heading for Blue Mills Landing. However, the scouts had not seen any sign of an approaching column of Union troops. Scott feared that the Sixteenth Illinois was late and that he would have no reinforcements, or, even worse, that the Illinois troops had arrived at the landing first, were waiting for Scott, and were in danger of being trapped against the river by the rebels. Trumbull described the night:

Before the men had finished their suppers, it was about ten o'clock, and once more they threw themselves on the ground to sleep. We all felt that it was the last night of campaigning for some of us, but who was to fall, was a secret yet wrapped in the gloom of the future. Col. Scott exquisitely sensitive about the honor of his regiment, was very restless all night, fearing that the enemy might escape, and that Col. Smith might be waiting for us, and in need of our assistance; so between one and two o'clock he gave orders to rouse the men and continue the march in order to reach Liberty (some ten miles distant) by daylight. The drums beat, the men sprang to their place, and away we went, through the dense, dark forest, the men cheering the dreary march by singing.... [3]

As the sun rose Scott and his men came to a steep hill that overlooked the town of Liberty. He anxiously scanned the roads with his field glasses but did not see the Illinois reinforcements. When he looked at the town he could see Confederate pickets posted on the outskirts. He knew that the rest of the enemy force was on its way to the landing. Some were probably already across the river or being ferried across. Scott had one chance to strike before the main body escaped—the perfect opportunity to catch the rebel army while it was divided. Scott heard cannon fire in the distance and thought it was either Colonel Smith and the Illinois troops trapped trying to hold the landing or a Union force on the other side of the river trying to stop the Confederates from crossing. Scott sent couriers to find the Illinois troops, if they were behind him, and tell them to hurry and that he was going to hold the rebels at the landing. If the Illinois troops were at the landing, the Iowa boys were on the way.[4]

Scott ordered his mounted Missouri loyalists ahead into town and they drove the Confederate pickets and rear guard through the streets of Liberty. The way now cleared, Scott marched his long column through the town on the narrow dirt road that led to the landing. Scott had no idea what was to his front as the thick trees and winding road obscured his view. Plus, his Missouri cavalry were still pursuing running pickets and had not returned with a report. He decided to push on. Neither Scott nor his cavalry knew that the Confederates were ready, standing in full force in the thick trees on both sides of the narrow dirt road.

Scott's Missouri horsemen kept up the pursuit, chasing the pickets toward the river, ignorant of the many rebels ahead. It was a bushwhacker's dream, a deadly crossfire. As the pickets raced past the hidden soldiers, the Missouri Unionists followed right behind and rode right into rebel gunfire. Four men were shot dead from their saddles; several others were wounded but kept their seats. The Missouri Yankees fired back and slowly retreated to the protection of Scott's column, bringing their wounded with them.[5]

When the cavalrymen retreated, the rebels took the bloody corpses of the four dead troopers and placed them in a row along the road as a warning to their pursuers. Scott and Major Stone led the infantry and were the first to see the bodies. Stone was appalled at the sight. One soldier described him as he "…stormed about in an excited manner and tried to prevent the boys from looking at the bodies. It was a ghastly sight, and calculated to unnerve us."[6]

Scott, on the other hand, had no such fears for the men's nerves. He wanted them to take a lesson. He marched them past the bodies, drew them to a battalion front, and had the men inspect their cartridges. He commanded them to load their smooth-bore Springfields and he rode along the line encouraging them and reminding them to fire low. He then called them into marching column again and took them forward, riding at their head with Trumbull and "I" Company close behind.

A Civil War marching formation was four men abreast, shoulder to shoulder, in a long column that crowded the narrow road and snaked back for miles. The thick trees and underbrush on both sides of the road made any kind of maneuver impossible. In the center, Scott placed his one artillery piece, pulled by two horses, and the gun's caisson, also pulled by two horses, both protected by Trumbull and the Union Guards. The rest of his cavalry was in the rear followed by the wagons. Trumbull and the other captains marched on foot with their men while Scott and Stone were mounted. The road wound through the heavily wooded Missouri River bottomland. Flankers struggled along in woods so thick that a soldier could hardly see to his front. Somewhere ahead, very close, was the enemy. Trumbull described the situation:

> The enemy was securely posted in a very strong position, a sort of dry creek bed forming a natural breastworks, which had been further strengthened and improved by logs and trees. His left flank was protected by a big slough, and his right by heavy timber. We had no room to work at all. We were in a narrow road, not wide enough indeed to allow our horses to turn conveniently when getting our gun into battery. We were marching up the road by the right flank, the flanks of the enemy almost encircling us in a giant's embrace….Company I was in front to protect the field piece, Company B was deployed as skirmishers on our left flank, Company G on our right, the rest of the regiment was strung along down the road.[7]

Lieutenant Colonel Scott was now aware that the enemy was out there, but he pressed forward anyway. If he feared that the rebels were crossing the river and escaping, the reverse was true. Whatever Confederate troops had crossed were ferried back and had joined their comrades in their hidden position. This was bushwhacking on a large scale.

As the Union troops approached, some men came out of the woods and waved them in. Scott halted the column, not sure who the men were. Scott forbade his men to fire and sent a party of twelve skirmishers under the command of Sergeant Jacob Abernathy of "F" Company forward to check it out. As they approached, the strangers disappeared back into the woods, and, at the same time, a full volley of musket fire exploded from the woods, wounding four of the skirmishers.

Scott reacted quickly. He ordered Trumbull and "I" Company forward into battle line and ordered the cannon forward. The gunners put the gun into action and fired two or three rounds of canister into the woods. The hidden rebels returned fire, dropping half the gunners and killing the gun's horses. The horses drawing the cannon's ammunition caisson panicked in the gunfire and took off, upsetting the caisson and dragging it behind them until it got stuck between two trees The screaming horses died in their harness.

The infantry returned fire, shooting at the bright red shirts of the enemy that showed through the smoky haze. Trumbull described the fight:

> Col. Scott on horseback in front of our battalion, was all through the engagement a conspicuous target for the enemy, but although his horse was shot no less than seven times, he miraculously escaped without a scratch. Our gun being almost within pigeon shot range of the enemy, the consequence was that our cannoneers and horses were soon killed off, and the gun became useless to us after the third round. Our men of course fell thick and fast, and fighting in such a shape necessarily could not observe much order. They kept loading and firing, however, with astonishing rapidity. When the enemy saw that our gun was silenced he made a charge down the road for the purpose of taking it, but was driven back with great loss by a well directed volley....[8]

As the rebels backed away from the abandoned cannon, Trumbull waved his sword, shouted for help, and ran forward. He was joined by Lieutenant John P. Knight, second in command of the Butler County Union Guards, Lieutenant George Crosley of "E" Company, Sergeant Jacob Abernathy of "F" Company, and one of the surviving sergeants from the gun's crew. The men took hold of the cannon and pulled it away by hand. Lieutenant Knight was hit three times—in the arm, the leg, and the face—but managed to stay with the gun and help drag it off. When they got the gun to safety, Trumbull, Crosley, and a few others ran forward again under fire to try to save the caisson. Trumbull cut the dead horses away but the caisson was too firmly wedged in the trees and they had to leave it.[9]

The fight at Blue Mills Landing lasted for less than an hour. During the fight, Major William Stone was hit, shot from his horse, and wounded in the head. He was taken to the rear where Dr. Daniel Cool treated his wound. But as fast as he could, Stone rounded up a wagon mule, mounted the animal, and, with his beard matted with blood and his head wrapped in a handkerchief, he returned to the fight. The Union troops slowly retreated, keeping good order, not letting the retreat become a rout. When Confederate troops tried to advance and sweep the road, Scott pulled together a rear guard, mostly of Fayette County boys from "E" and "F" companies, that held its ground until the main body retired safely. One of the rear guard, Sergeant James Lakin of "F" Company defiantly waved the company's flag, a gift from the ladies of Fayette County. There was no more pursuit and both sides backed away.[10]

Scott wanted to reform the men and charge back down the road, but it was nearly dark and the men were exhausted. Major Stone managed to convince Scott to take the men back to Liberty. The Confederates held the battlefield and were able to ferry their troops across the Missouri with no more opposition. That night, after Scott's men got back to Liberty, Colonel Smith and the Sixteenth Illinois arrived.

The next morning Scott sent his Missouri cavalry back to Blue Mills Landing to reconnoiter. The battlefield was empty; the Confederates were gone. The rest of the day was spent caring for the wounded and burying the dead. The William Jewell College in Liberty became the hospital.

Scott lost one hundred and eighteen men, killed and wounded, and ninety-four of them were from his Third Iowa. It was the hardest day of the war for Trumbull's Union Guards. One out of four of the men Trumbull had recruited had been shot, three had been killed, and twenty-five had been wounded.[11] In his official report, Scott gave special mention to Captain Trumbull and "I" Company for their gallant conduct.[12]

Lieutenant Colonel Scott received much criticism for getting his men into the fight, but most also commended him for his bravery and coolness under fire. Matthew Trumbull, in spite of the loss of so many of his men, publicly supported Scott's decision:

> It may be asked, why did Lieut. Col. Scott give battle with his small force to an enemy so much stronger, and entrenched in a strong position, and why did he not wait for Col. Smith? I answer, we had been ordered to prevent the enemy from crossing the river. He was already at the crossing place. To wait until Col. Smith should come, would give him ample time to get over. By engaging him there was a chance of keeping him employed until Col. Smith's arrival....
>
> It may be asked why fight them on their own ground, and under their own entrenchments? I answer, we were right on them before we knew it; we were in an ambuscade. To get out, there was but one way, fight out, and we did so. To have attempted to get out by a retreat in such a narrow road, would have had a bad moral influence on the men; it would have thrown us into confusion; it would have given the enemy time to play upon our retreating men, without getting anything in return. We had to fight out, there was no other way.
>
> Our commanding officer, Col. Scott, proved himself in this fight to be a cool brave man, and a true soldier. He was in the front all the time, and was literally "the first in the field and the last in the fight."[13]

CHAPTER 8

The Battle of Pittsburg Landing (Shiloh)

The Battle of Blue Mills was the last major campaign in Missouri for the Third Iowa Infantry. The regiment went into the state over one thousand strong in June 1861 and by September, without having fought a battle, only five hundred men were healthy enough to march to Blue Mills. After that battle, Matthew Trumbull explained the reasons for the depleted condition of the Third Iowa:

> In the first place we went into Missouri poorly equipped,...In the next place we were immediately detailed in for duty guarding railroad bridges at different places along the line of the Hannibal and St. Jo railroad. The whole of this country is unhealthy, especially to strangers, and the bridges being, of course, over rivers and creeks we were mostly encamped on the bottoms, among the stagnant pools and sloughs. In addition to this, the men were often left for days, without tents, a change of clothing, or anything to cook their provisions in. Besides the provisions themselves were often inferior in quality, and scant in quantity....All this time the men would be tramping from county to county under the sweltering sun, and at night lie down on the ground to sleep under the heaviest dews I ever saw, with nothing but a blanket to cover them....Of course, under such hard labor as this many men are on the sick report. These are some of the reasons why the Third Iowa Regiment was so greatly reduced in its effective members.[1]

The Third Iowa was moved around that summer and fall from Macon City to Kansas City and finally, in October, sent to Quincy, Illinois, for rest and refitting. The men enjoyed their stay at Quincy. Leaves and furloughs were granted, daily drill was reduced to just a few hours, and no patrols or picket duties were required. The men received five months back pay and, at long last, issued regulation blue Yankee uniforms. The uniforms were, however, of poor quality, much worse than their old dragoon uniforms which the men had grown to like. What really angered the men was that when the new uniforms were issued, they were required to turn in their gray uniforms and $15.00 was deducted from their pay for the old uniforms. (Complaints over having to pay for the uniforms were effective. The Iowa legislature passed a resolution to reimburse the $15.00. Long after the war, the Iowa Adjutant General's files contained many letters from veterans and widows asking for their $15.00 back.)[2]

In early November, the regiment was ordered to Benton Barracks, Missouri. Benton Barracks was the largest permanent military camp in the Western theater of the war. It was constructed under the orders of Major General John Charles Frémont and named for his father-in-law, Thomas Hart Benton, the most powerful Republican in Missouri. The camp was located at the old fairgrounds on the outskirts of St. Louis, about four miles from the levee. The camp covered several acres and was large enough for full battalions to be quartered and drilled. It had long rows of whitewashed barracks, two storied buildings for the officers, and a full parade ground. On the east end was the headquarters of the commanding general, William Strong, a personal friend of John C. Frémont.[3]

Benton Barracks was thoroughly military. Few passes were given and almost constant drill and hard duty were required. The barracks were crowded and the men were forced to sleep in berths covered with straw that was often infested with ticks and fleas. Lieutenant Thompson described life there:

> From *reveille* till *retreat* there was a constant hubbub pervading this little city, and the interior square presented a scene of splendid confusion. The noises of bugles, drums, and voices commanding; infantry, cavalry, and artillery, drilling by the multitude....
>
> Such was Benton Barracks. Without, the pomp of marching battalions, and galloping squadrons, and batteries; within, the discomfort of men, poorly fed, poorly lodged, and jostled against each other continually in darkness and foul air.[4]

Lieutenant Colonel Scott remained in command because Colonel Nelson Williams was still under house arrest in St. Louis. Charges had been brought against him in August but he had not yet received a trial. The colonel repeatedly denied the charges and demanded his day in court. In a letter to Iowa Assistant Adjutant General Captain P. E. Hall, Williams said: "...I say on the honor of a man, that the charges against me are false, and that I am the victim of malignant enemies."[5]

Williams's supporters also demanded a trial. Governor Kirkwood tried to intervene. In a letter to General Frémont, he demanded that Williams be given his trial, saying: "If the charges be true I hope Col. Williams will be promptly disciplined, if untrue he has suffered a grievous harm which should be righted."[6]

Even John Scott, no friend of Williams, wrote to General Frémont seeking resolution: "This regiment has been without the services of its proper commander for two months and nineteen days and its efficiency necessarily impaired thereby."[7]

The trial had originally been scheduled for September, but the Blue Mills campaign prevented it as no officers of the Third Iowa could leave the field to testify. The trial was rescheduled, but it was discovered that the papers specifying the original charges were lost. Without those critical documents a court martial could not be held. Williams and his supporters did not want the trial canceled on a technicality;

they wanted vindication. In November 1861 General Henry W. Halleck replaced General Frémont as commanding officer of the Missouri district. On 2 December, Williams wrote to Halleck on the subject of his trial and the lost papers:

> General—Understanding that the original papers containing charges against me are lost or mislaid. I hereby relinquish all claims I may have to be tried upon the original paper. I also waive all technicalities that can possibly arise, and earnestly request that I may be tried upon a copy of said charges.[8]

Three days later General Halleck issued this order:

> The records of this office show that *Col. N. Williams* 3rd Iowa regiment Volunteers, has long been in arrest without trial. From a copy of the charges on file it seems that they were of a serious character, but as no originals can be found it becomes necessary that *Col. Williams* be released from arrest and will immediately join his regiment for duty.[9]

However, being released from arrest was not what Williams wanted, and he again applied to Halleck for a formal court martial. Halleck ignored the request and ordered that Williams return to his duties as colonel of the Third Iowa.[10]

Colonel Williams went from his St. Louis hotel to Benton Barracks, once more in command of the regiment but in no mind to mend fences or forget the past. Lieutenant S. D. Thompson wrote: "Immediately on assuming command, he arrested a number of officers, his personal enemies."[11] Thompson did not say which officers Williams placed under arrest, but it hardly mattered. Although the colonel may have believed that he was in his rights to order the arrests, he had broken military protocol. Williams was in command of the regiment, but General Strong commanded Benton Barracks, and he took a dim view of Williams's actions. General Strong canceled the arrest orders and complained to General Halleck about the colonel.

Halleck responded to this latest incident concerning Williams by revoking the colonel's release and ordering that he be put on trial on the original charges, papers or not. Halleck ordered Williams to report to General Strong, under arrest, again. Williams, having received exactly what he had originally requested, obeyed Halleck's order and was sent back to St. Louis.

The trial lasted for two months. John Scott, Matthew Trumbull, Thomas Edwards, Richard Herron, and many others were called to testify. The court also received letters and telegrams from Williams's supporters. Williams made a better impression on the officers of the court than he had on his own officers. In February 1862, the court ruled in Williams's favor and ordered him to resume command of his regiment. The *Dubuque Daily Times* said this about his acquittal:

The numerous friends of this gentleman will be gratified to know that he has been found "not guilty" of any of the charges or specifications against him....

We find that the court martial honorably acquitted him, and that the finding has been approved by the Major General, and Colonel Williams ordered to resume his sword.[12]

On 25 February 1862 Colonel Williams's train arrived at Mexico, Missouri, the latest regimental headquarters of the Third Iowa. (The Third had left Benton Barracks on Christmas Day.) A formation of troops from "K" and "F" Companies met Williams at the station. The men of "K" Company (Black Hawk County) greeted the colonel with proper military courtesy and enthusiastic cheers. But the men of "F" Company (Fayette County) were not as respectful, and the insult of "Shelbina!" was heard from their ranks.[13]

Even Williams's harshest critics agreed that the strict discipline and attention to drill that he required was better for the regiment than the other officers' leniency in such matters. The "K" Company soldier, known as Udonohu, wrote to the *Cedar Falls Gazette*:

I am not certain that the want of restraint and discipline has been really of much benefit to the Regiment. Without casting any reflection upon any officer in the Regiment, I think that in point of discipline, the Regiment have taken a backward move since the arrest of Col. Williams, and for one, I shall be glad to see him at the head of his men again.[14]

This time Colonel Williams did not initiate a purge of his enemies, and most of his officers and men seemed willing to give him another chance. John Scott, Williams's chief opponent, was home on furlough due to the death of his wife, and Major Stone was now second in command. Lieutenant S. D. Thompson wrote:

We hoped that his long arrest had furnished an opportunity for meditation and repentance, and that he would be more careful in his conduct now. This was the case. Before his arrival we did everything slackly. We almost began to forget that we were soldiers. The first thing he did was to enforce discipline. He instituted regular roll-calls, drills twice a day, and daily dress parades. He did nothing that we could complain of, though we watched him with the eyes of cynics. Day by day our former prejudices against him began to wear away. Almost imperceptibly those hitherto antagonistic elements, the colonel and his men, began to harmonize. Colonel Williams was a wiser officer, and we were better soldiers.[15]

(Richard Herron of "A" Company was an exception to the harmony and resigned shortly after Williams returned.)[16]

Williams's newfound success with the regiment was rewarded. In the spring of 1862, without receiving an actual promotion, by special order of General Stephen

Hurlbut he was placed in command of the First Brigade, Fourth Division, of the Army of the Tennessee. The brigade was made up of the three Illinois infantry regiments, the Third Iowa infantry, and a battery of light artillery—a truly fine command for the once disgraced colonel.[17]

Williams's advance resulted in similar advances in the Third Iowa. Lieutenant Colonel John Scott, now back with the regiment, took command once more, though he, too, had not received an actual promotion. William Stone, still a major, did the duties of lieutenant colonel, and Matthew Trumbull, still a captain, became the acting major.

The Southern Confederacy was separated from the United States by a line of defenses that roughly stretched along the Ohio River from Virginia to the Mississippi River. Union strategy was to smash through the Ohio River line at some place and invade the rebel states.

THE UNION INVASION OF THE TENNESSEE VALLEY

The Battle of Pittsburg Landing (Shiloh)

The first break in the Confederate line came in Tennessee. Two rebel forts, Fort Henry and Fort Donelson, commanded the Tennessee and Cumberland Rivers, the natural invasion routes to the South. In February 1862, General U. S. Grant captured the forts and began a river-based invasion of the South. Using the Tennessee River as a highway, Grant drove his Army of the Tennessee deep into the Confederacy, establishing a series of military camps and hospitals from Savannah to Pittsburg Landing, Tennessee. General Grant had over forty thousand troops under his command and was expecting 20,000 more men under General Don Carlos Buell and up to 15,000 more under General Lew Wallace. Once his three forces were united, Grant planned to leave the landing and drive deeper into the South.

If the Confederacy was going to survive, Grant's army had to be destroyed quickly before it was united. To that end, the largest Confederate army ever assembled was ready. Forty thousand men organized into four corps at Corinth, Mississippi, less than twenty miles southwest of Grant's encampment. The army was under the command of General Albert Sidney Johnston, the most admired officer in the South. Second to him were Generals Braxton Bragg and P. G. T. Beauregard. They were aggressive generals under pressure from Richmond and the whole South to drive the invaders out. They intended to strike at Grant before he could be reinforced.

In March the Third Iowa was ordered to leave Mexico, Missouri, and was transported by steamboat to St. Louis and then to Fort Henry, Tennessee. Grant's army had already left the fort but he still had his headquarters there. When the Third Iowa arrived, the men heard rumors that Grant was planning something big and that Hurlbut's division and Williams's new brigade were going to be part of it. On March 17 the Third Iowa got off the boats at Pittsburg Landing.

The Pittsburg Landing camps were big: acre after acre of military tents, officers' wall tents, and enlisted men's Sibley tents. (The two-man "dog-tent" came later in the war.) Acre after acre of artillery, guns, caissons, and endless picket lines of horses stretched across the fields behind the guns. Thousands of soldiers drilled, paraded, stood guard, played horseshoes, read, cooked, and generally lived the lives of soldiers in camp. Some women were also in the camp. Officers' wives came and went freely, and some female nurses tended the sick. After his victories at Henry and Donelson, U.S. Grant was fast becoming the rising military star in the West, so reporters and politicians were frequent sights.

The camps were on the west bank of the Tennessee River not far from a small Christian meeting house called Shiloh Church. It was the only place suitable for such a large body of men, horses, and guns. The camps stretched almost three miles along the banks of the river and almost three miles inland. The camps had their back to the spring-swollen river and their flanks firmly anchored on Owl Creek and Lick Creek, with a two and a half mile picket line that faced toward Corinth. The landing allowed Union boats to debark troops and supplies easily and to just as efficiently ship sick soldiers upriver to Grant's hospitals at Savannah. Hospital boats also floated on the river allowing sick soldiers to be treated close to camp. The gunboats on the river were Grant's floating artillery that had been critical to his victories at Fort Henry and Fort Donelson.

However, these were unhealthy camps. The rain and drizzle of March and early April, combined with the marching feet of thousands of troops, the wheels of thousands of wagons and caissons, and the hoof prints and manure droppings of countless horses and mules, turned the roads, paths, and drill fields into muddy pits. The shallow wells flooded, and the slit trench latrine system was inadequate. The hospitals were crowded. Lieutenant Colonel John Scott, for one, had fallen sick with fever and rested onboard one of the hospital boats.

The camps were also not secure. There were no trenches, no fortifications, no real plan of defense. The most experienced of Grant's veteran regiments were camped in the rear, while his newest regiments were camped just behind the front pickets. The Third Iowa, for example, was camped at Stacy Field, less than half a mile from the river, and close to two miles from the front picket line.

Grant, in his memoirs, confessed that he did not expect to be attacked:

> The fact is, I regarded the campaign we were engaged in as an offensive one and had no idea that the enemy would leave strong entrenchments to take the initiative when he knew he would be attacked where he was if he remained.[18]

General Grant's most trusted subordinate was General William T. Sherman, who commanded a division at the front of Grant's line and kept his headquarters near the Shiloh meeting house. Sherman, too, did not expect an attack and had fiercely berated anyone who dared suggest that there was any large Confederate force this side of Corinth.

Grant and Sherman may have been confident, but others were not—there had been warnings. On Friday night, 4 April, a fierce thunderstorm forced the troops to take shelter in their crowded tents where they tried to sleep. Just as things settled down in camp, Captain Matthew Trumbull and the rest of the Third Iowa were wakened by the sound of the long roll, the infantryman's call to arms. The drums were not from his camp but Trumbull quickly dressed and raced out of his tent where he found most of his men already up, dressed, and close to their weapons. Just then General Hurlbut rode into camp, shouting for the drummers to pick up on the long roll. He called out to Major Stone that Sherman was under attack and that the Third was going to his aid. Stone signaled Captain Trumbull who then ordered the men to take arms and fall in. With Stone and Trumbull riding at the head of the column, the men marched out through the rain into the muddy darkness. They marched for almost three-quarters of a mile toward Sherman's line before they were halted. A courier from Hurlbut informed Major Stone that there was no attack. Sherman's pickets had clashed with some rebel cavalry, but there was no attack. Major Stone and Captain Trumbull marched the men back to camp.[19]

The next day, Saturday, was sunny with peach blossoms scenting the air. The men were allowed to relax in their camps. There was much talk of the last night's mud march. Few of the men liked General Hurlbut; most believed that had he failed Colonel Williams at Shelbina because he had been drunk. "All aboard for Shelbina!" was a common catcall thrown at the general. Now it seemed obvious that he had been drunk again and had sent them out on a wet, silly exercise.

Several transport boats landed during the day and brought more troops. Among the new arrivals was the Sixteenth Iowa Infantry, a new regiment that had only received its muskets the day before. The new troops had to be drilled as quickly as possible. They were sent to General Benjamin Prentiss whose division was camped as far from the river as possible and had the driest and least used parade ground.

Prentiss's camp was close to the front pickets and close to Sherman's camp near Shiloh Church. The Iowa soldiers got their first instructions with their new weapons and learned some drill. That night they slept well, looking forward to a long Sunday in camp.

At dawn, Sunday morning, Confederate General Albert Sidney Johnston conferred with Bragg and Beauregard and mounted his big horse to inspect his battle lines of thousands of Confederate soldiers ready to attack. His was a new army with few veteran regiments, and its march north from Corinth had not been as secretive as it needed to be. The men had practiced their rebel yells, fired their weapons, crashed through the woods, and tramped about noisily on the muddy roads. Johnston feared that Grant's scouts had heard the noise, seen the troops, and informed their general. If Grant knew what was coming, his camp would be strongly fortified. But Confederate luck held; Grant's camp was open. General Johnston looked at his officers and said, "Tonight, gentlemen, we will water our horses in the Tennessee River." He then sent his army forward.

Sherman was at his headquarters when he heard his pickets firing. He called for his horse and, at the head of his staff, rode to the front. The advance of the attack was less than a hundred yards beyond his pickets with gray-clad soldiers as far as he could see. The advance rebel skirmishers halted at a small stream in front of Sherman, raised their muskets, aimed, and fired. Sherman's orderly dropped dead from his saddle, and Sherman took a bullet through his hand. He wrapped the wound and turned to rally his men. The battle had started.

The Confederates came in waves, striking at Prentiss's and Sherman's divisions first, overrunning their camps. The new regiments took the first hit; the Sixteenth Iowa was all but destroyed in a few minutes.

Trumbull and his men were well to the rear, expecting a comfortable Sunday. The rain had stopped and it looked to be a pleasant day. The smell of campfires and food being cooked filled the air. While the men ate their breakfast, Trumbull heard gunfire, cannon fire, and infantry volley fire in the distance but it was far too heavy to be merely pickets skirmishing. Trumbull ordered the long drum roll to be beaten and the men ran for their stacks of muskets. Major Stone and Captain Trumbull hurried the men into formation first as companies, then as a regiment, and then in their proper place in the brigade's marching order. The men were told to load their smoothbore Springfields with buck and ball for what promised to be a close range fight. Colonel Williams and Adjutant Fitzroy Sessions led the brigade forward; Stone and Trumbull led the Third Iowa.

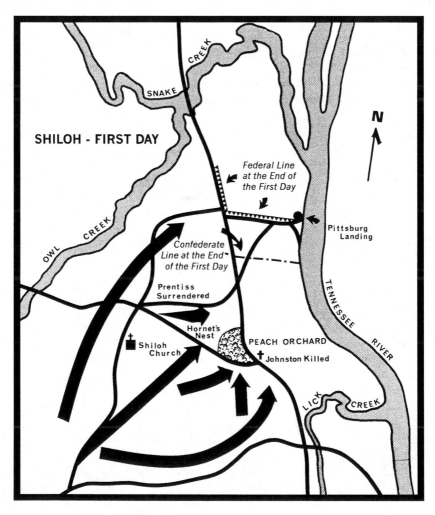

The Battle of Pittsburg Landing (Shiloh)

As they marched forward on the muddy roads into the tangled woods and small clearings, they heard the firing grow more intense. They traveled almost a mile when they saw the first of the wounded and retreating men. Private John H. Kellenbarger of "B" Company, a new recruit who had joined the regiment at Benton Barracks, described the scene.

> Some who were wounded in the hand, arms, or head, and could walk were assisting others who were wounded in the feet or legs and couldn't walk alone. Some were on horses, some in wagons, some in ambulances and all covered over more or less with blood. Some were groaning and moaning and making a dreadful noise. From these fellows we frequently heard such exclamations as, "You won't keep such order as them when you get out there!" "We are all cut to pieces!" "Our Regiment is gone to hell!"[20]

Some men shouted insults at the fleeing soldiers, calling them cowards and deserters, but Major Stone silenced them, saying there was no time for that. Williams took the brigade forward and reported to Hurlbut, who was getting his whole division into place. Lieutenant S. D. Thompson described the sight of the mounting reinforcements.

> It was a glorious, an all cheering sight, battalion after battalion moving on in splendid order, stemming the tide of these broken masses; not a man straggling; regiments seeming to be animated by one soul. These were the troops of the Fourth Division....[21]

By eight in the morning, Williams's brigade was a part of the rear guard. To its front the brigade was protected from infantry fire by a small wooded ridge, but it was still exposed to rebel artillery firing randomly over the ridge. The officers remained on their horses but Major Stone ordered the men to lie down in their ranks and take what cover they could find as shells burst in the branches above them and cannon balls smashed into the trees, fences, and dirt around them.

Orders came to shift position and the brigade was hurried forward to one of several cotton fields scattered in clearings throughout the woods. To their front the men saw two cannons abandoned earlier in the battle. Further across the field they finally saw the rebel troops. Lieutenant S. D. Thompson wrote of that moment.

> Beyond the field, we for the first time caught sight of the enemy, his regiments with their red banners flashing in the morning sun marching proudly and all undisturbed through the abandoned camps of Prentiss.[22]

Hurlbut shifted the brigade again, moving it from a rear guard position to the front of the battle line where it directly faced rebel infantry and cannon fire. The men of the Third got off one volley before the enemy guns went into action. At first the cannon fire was high, hitting the trees and dropping limbs and branches onto the men, but the gunners soon found the range and the cannon shot got closer. Colonel Williams, mounted on his big sorrel horse, rode bravely along his lines, encouraging the men. Suddenly a solid shot came screaming by, smashed into Williams's horse and cut the animal in two. Williams flew from the saddle and landed, unconscious, next to the bloody carcass. Fitzroy Sessions galloped his mount forward, dismounted, and dragged the colonel to safety.[23]

Major Stone then ordered the men to lie down again, and for over an hour they lay there listening to the sounds of battle. When the battery stopped firing Stone and Trumbull ordered the men to rise and fire one volley, then two volleys. It was about ten o'clock when General Grant arrived with a few of his staff officers and rode by the men of the Third Iowa on his way to check on Sherman and Prentiss. The Third Iowa troops started to raise a cheer for the general, but Stone and Trumbull ordered them to be silent so as not to draw fire.

Grant was not at the landing when the battle started but rather was upriver at his supply base and hospitals at Savannah. He had been hurt and was moving slowly that morning. His horse had slipped and fallen on a muddy road the night before, pinning him beneath it. No bones were broken, but Grant needed crutches. When messengers brought him news of the dawn attack, Grant returned to Pittsburg Landing as soon as possible. S. D. Thompson described him as he rode by, his crutches strapped to his saddle.

The general's countenance wore an anxious look, yet bore no evidence of excitement or trepidation. He rode leisurely forward to the front line. We did not see him again till night.[24]

The Confederate attack seemed to be unstoppable; the whole Union line was pushed back. Williams's brigade, now commanded by Colonel Isaac C. Pugh of Illinois, was forced to retreat. At the height of the crisis, Grant's army was saved by the heroism of General Benjamin Prentiss and the soldiers that rallied to him.

Prentiss's division was routed from its camps at the start of the battle and the men ran back toward the river. It was not all a panic as Prentiss succeeded in rallying many

Benjamin M. Prentiss
(*Drawing by Ron Prahl*)

of his troops and brought some order to the retreat. When he found an old wagon trail, rutted and sunken by years of use, he called a halt, stopped the retreat, and ordered what was left of his division to take cover in the road and be ready to defend it. A brigade of five Iowa regiments soon joined Prentiss and he placed them in the center of his line. He had over two thousand men ready when the rebels struck. The charging rebels were met with a "hornet's nest" of gunfire and fell back. Again and again they charged, and each time Prentiss's men held the road. This Hornet's Nest was the battle within the larger battle that slowed the Confederate advance and saved the day for the Union.

When Prentiss made his stand in the sunken road, General Hurlbut moved to support him and protect the left of the Hornet's Nest. Hurlbut set his line at the edge of a peach orchard that faced a cotton field. Private John Kellenbarger described the part the Third Iowa played as they fought along a rail fence at Hurlbut's orchard.

> This was a good position for us, for the rail fence caught many of the balls that would have played havoc with our ranks....The Rebels were on one side of this field and we were on the other, with a ridge in the middle so we could just see their heads, I guess there was twenty-five or thirty rods between us....We loaded our guns and waited till the Johnnies were near enough when we would take aim from the fence and let them have it, and then back they would go, that is, what was left of them. Finally after waiting quite a while to reform, here they would come again thicker and faster than before, shooting as they came, with bayonets fixed, intending to charge and drive us back from the fence....This last time we waited till they got well over the ridge and then let them have a well directed volley aimed from the top of the fences; the batteries also gave it to them rapidly. As soon as the smoke cleared, we could see apparently about half of them disappearing over the ridge. The dead and the mortally wounded we could now see thickly lying all through the middle of the field. Occasionally a Johnnie who had been stunned, or slightly wounded, would get up from among the dead and attempt to run, walk, or crawl off, but a dozen well-directed shots from us would bring him down, to rise no more.[25]

Confederate General Albert Sidney Johnston saw that the Union line at the Hornet's Nest and the peach orchard had slowed his attack. It was getting later in the day and he was still a long way from the river. He decided to sweep around the Hornet's Nest, flanking it on both sides. To do this, Johnston stopped the attacks on the sunken road and brought his reserves to the right and left of Prentiss's Hornet's Nest. Johnston was right across the cotton field from the Third Iowa, riding up and down the line to steady his men for the attack, calling for them to use their bayonets.

Major Stone and Captain Trumbull sat on their horses watching at least a full rebel brigade forming in front of them. General Hurlbut and Adjutant Sessions were nearby, also watching Johnston massing his troops. Hurlbut rode over to Major Stone

William M. Stone
(*Drawing by Ron Prahl*)

and told him that he had to hold that position no matter what. Stone gave the same order to Trumbull.

Johnston sent his Confederates forward, hitting both flanks of Prentiss's line. But Hurlbut's brigade was ready as the Third Iowa and the other regiments fired volley after volley, forcing the rebels back. Johnston reformed his men, determined to smash through. This time he led them across the bloody field in person. As the rebels charged, Hurlbut saw that they couldn't be stopped. He galloped over to Major Stone, canceled his previous order, and told the major to fall back. As Stone's men retreated, General Johnston's men surged forward, drove the Union troops from the orchard, and took it for their own. General Johnston was mortally wounded while leading the successful attack. Hurlbut's retreat forced General Prentiss to abandon the Hornet's Nest and fall back. Prentiss tried to keep his line intact to buy time as he slowly retreated and hoped the rest of the Union troops would form a new line to his rear.

Stone and Trumbull took their men back about three hundred yards and stopped, reformed, faced about, and fired full volleys at the advancing Confederates. Prentiss stopped his retreat when he found the Third Iowa bravely holding its new position. He rode to Major Stone and ordered the Third Iowa to hold its place as he formed his division on the Third's flank. Together they formed a new front. The new line held for over an hour, throwing back repeated charges. But by 5:00 p.m., the Confederates had caved in both flanks and the line fell apart as the two wings of rebels closed in.

Stone ordered his men to retreat. They raced for their lives and took cover at their Stacy Field camp. Stone sent Adjutant Sessions to the left of the camp and Trumbull to the center while he held the right, hoping to keep the Third Iowa intact and use it for a rallying point.

The attempt failed. The men could not rally and the enemy closed in on three sides. Their only hope was to get to the river. It was every man for himself, no orders, no commands. Private Kellenbarger explained.

> The rebels were out-numbering and out-maneuvering us now and we could plainly see that very soon their two wings would come together and we would be prisoners of war. Major Stone commanded the Regiment to retreat down the road to our old camp, so we ceased firing and ran the gauntlet between the two Rebel

wings, that were loading and firing at us as they advanced. Many loose horses, caissons, artillery wagons, ambulances…were rushing out through the gap and we had to keep close watch or they would run over us.[26]

Adjutant Sessions made it to the river first where he and the men with him tried to throw together a defensive line. Major Stone tried to retreat through the old camp and run for shelter in the woods but was cut off. Stone's horse was killed and, as he fell to the ground, he was surrounded; he and thirty men of the Third Iowa were captured. Stone surrendered his sword to Colonel William H. Rankin of Mississippi.

Captain Trumbull took command of what was left of the regiment and tried to get to the river. However, a shell burst over his head, knocked him from his horse, and wounded him in the head and thigh. Lieutenant George W. Crosley of E Company, in his war memoir, described what happened next:

Just after we had passed our camp ground the brave Captain M. M. Trumbull… was wounded, and fell immediately in front of me. I stopped and raised him to a sitting posture, but he insisted upon my leaving him, saying it was better for him to be captured than for me to share his fate. Just then Joseph McGinnis—a large and powerful soldier of Captain Trumbull's company (I)—came to the rescue, shouldering his captain and bore him to a place of safety in the rear.[27]

General Prentiss was cornered in a place called Hell's Hollow where he finally mounted the stump of a tree, waved a white handkerchief, and also surrendered his sword to Mississippi's Colonel Rankin.[28]

Everything was confusion back at the river. Hundreds of fear-crazed men cowered beneath the river bluffs. Others were too afraid to stay on land and jumped into the fast moving water, trying to make it to the safety of the boats. Many of them drowned trying. Officers such as Trumbull and Sessions desperately tried to pull the panicked men into one last defensive line. Trumbull, though staggering weakly with his wounds, kept command of the regiment. On the water, Grant's gunboats acted as artillery support and sent hundreds of shells over the heads of the union troops and into the oncoming rebels.

The line at the river's edge was the last line. If it fell, the rebels would be able to water their horses in the Tennessee. The line held. Darkness finally came, the fighting stopped, and the rebel troops fell back to the captured camps. They started to dig in and prepare for the next day when they were sure to finish what they had started that morning.

It rained again that night. An April rain that was cold and fierce, accompanied by crashing thunder and lightning flashes that lit the night, exposing the bloody battlefield. Grant kept his gunboats firing all night and the sounds and bright flashes of cannon fire joined the thunder and lightning.

During the night the first of Grant's promised reinforcements arrived by transport boats—a whole new army under General Buell. All night long thousands of blue-coated soldiers, fresh and ready, came off the boats.

If the first day's fighting was the story of Union resistance, the story of the second day was one of Confederate resistance. With fresh troops, Grant was determined to win back all that he had lost and to inflict as much damage on the enemy as possible. He succeeded. Braxton Bragg and P. G. T. Beauregard were forced to take what was left of their great army back to Corinth. General Johnston was left behind, buried near where he died.

The Third Iowa played a rear guard role in the second day of fighting and only came under fire for a few brief moments. Matthew Trumbull's wound kept him in the field hospital and he gave command to Lieutenant George W. Crosley.

The battle was over; the greatest Union victory in the war was won but at a staggering cost. Grant lost over 13,000 men, killed and wounded, and the Confederates lost over 10,000.[29]

The Third Iowa lost 187 men. Twenty-three were killed, 134 were wounded, and the rest were missing, most of them captured with Major Stone. Twenty-one of the casualties were from Trumbull's Butler County Union Guards—two were dead, nineteen wounded, and the wounded Lieutenant John P. Knight was captured.[30]

Trumbull resumed command of the regiment a day later, and on 17 April 1861 he submitted the official report of the battle to General Hurlbut.

> Sir: I have the honor to report the part taken by the Third Iowa Infantry in the action of the 6th and 7th instant.
>
> The Third Iowa occupied the extreme right of the Fourth Division, being the first regiment of Col. and Actg. Brig. Gen. N. G. Williams' brigade, and was posted during a greater portion of Sunday at the fence near the cotton field. The enemy repeatedly threw large bodies of infantry against us, but never with success. He was repulsed every time with great slaughter. The regiment was also subjected to a storm of grape, canister, and shell, which lasted several hours. The Third Iowa maintained its ground until evening and did not give way until the troops on their right and left had broken and we were entirely outflanked and almost surrounded. The regiment was then compelled in a great measure to cut its way out.
>
> Of the firmness, coolness, and courage of the men under fire it will be unnecessary for me to speak, as they were almost constantly during the battle under the immediate eye of the general commanding the division.
>
> The regiment went into battle on the second day under the command of First Lieut. G. W. Crosley, of Company E, and, as I am well assured, nobly maintained the honor of the flag.
>
> Should I designate meritorious officers I should have to name nearly every officer in the regiment. I think, however, none will feel envious if I especially mention Lieutenant Crosley.

The Battle of Pittsburg Landing (Shiloh)

I desire to call the attention of the general commanding the division to the gallantry and good conduct of Sergt. James Lakin, of Company F, who carried the colors on the first day, and of Corp. Anderson Edwards, of Company I, who carried the colors the second day, of the battle.

Our loss is heavy. I herewith inclose a list of our killed and wounded.

I have the honor to remain, sir, very respectfully, your obedient servant.

M. M. Trumbull

Captain, Third Iowa Infantry, Commanding Regiment [31]

CHAPTER 9

The Hero of the Hatchie

General Ulysses S. Grant won a great victory at Pittsburg Landing (Shiloh), but its importance as a victory was obscured by how close he came to losing the fight. A surprise attack by a full Confederate army certainly reflected poorly on the commanding officer. Although the nighttime arrival of reinforcements had rescued his army, hard feelings against Grant remained. A private in "K" Company, Third Iowa Infantry, expressed what the soldiers thought:

> They knew that there was a large army pitted against them, commanded by the best generals in the Southern Confederacy, and the first question they asked themselves was, "Are we commanded by a man who has allowed the enemy to steal up on us unawares?" If this be generalship, in the calm of a tented field, what will it be in battle? There was hardly a soldier or officer in the army that did not expect that Beauregard would make an attack on us. . . [1]

Public outcry against the general who was surprised in his own camps forced President Lincoln to react. For the time being, Grant was replaced by General Halleck as the field commander of the Army of the Tennessee.

The battle damaged Grant's reputation but, in other cases, the battle enhanced reputations. Most of the men of the Third Iowa had not wanted to be under General Stephen Hurlbut's command. They blamed Hurlbut for the Shelbina affair and were ready to believe that he was a drunkard. Hurlbut's magnificent performance at Shiloh changed all that. His Friday night mud march proved that he was aware of the enemy's presence, and the men noted his bravery and skill in handling his division on both days of the battle. A Third Iowa sergeant said, "...it is

Stephen A. Hurlbut
(*Drawing by Ron Prahl*)

due to Hurlbut to say that for once he was not drunk, and that he performed his part well."[2] Lieutenant S. D. Thompson was even more succinct.

> The battle changed materially the morale of the army. It had diminished our inclination to boast. If it had not taught us to respect ourselves less, it had taught us to respect our enemies more. It diminished our confidence in General Grant, and greatly increased it in Hurlbut….The conduct of the latter won our unbounded admiration. We had expected nothing of him; he had done everything for us. If the country did not know it, we nevertheless felt it—that the Fourth Division under his leadership had covered itself with glory.[3]

Shiloh might have done the same for Colonel Nelson Williams. The shadow of his trial was still there, but General Hurlbut had shown confidence in Williams by giving him a new brigade. The brigade was filled with experienced troops, and Williams had seen to it that the men were well-equipped, well-drilled, and healthy. If he and the brigade could distinguish themselves, his reputation would have been salvaged. However, battle luck ruined Williams's chance. Just as he and his brigade became involved in the battle, Williams was wounded and taken out of the fight. No one knows how Williams would have performed at the peach orchard or during the desperate retreat.

Williams was granted a furlough after the battle and returned to his Iowa farm to recuperate. To the citizens of Dyersville, Colonel Williams was a hometown hero, and they welcomed him back with a grand reception at the town hall. *The Dubuque Daily Times* published this account:

> He gave a modest but graphic account of the great battle, and one that thrilled the hearts of the hearers. Especially did the account of his own disaster….
>
> His position in Missouri, while made the object of the envy and malice of his enemies, his complete vindication from all the charges brought against him, had awakened strong sympathy among his fellow citizens, and his return after the almost miraculous escape had awakened still more the public interest in him. He was repeatedly and enthusiastically cheered during his remarks, and the thanks of the audience for them was given in three enthusiastic cheers.[4]

After a few weeks leave Williams reported himself fit for duty. He had lost his brigade command in the restructuring of the Army of the Tennessee after Shiloh and was ordered to once more take command of the Third Iowa.

Lieutenant Colonel John Scott, barely recovered from his fever, would not serve under Williams's immediate command again and submitted his resignation in early June. Scott was an unabashed glory hunter and political animal. He returned to Iowa where he attended the Republican State Convention and campaigned for the party's nomination to congress from his district. He failed in the attempt, partly because

Black Hawk County was in the district. The nominating delegates from Black Hawk did not forgive him for what he had done to Colonel Williams and refused to endorse him. Scott then appealed to his friend, Governor Kirkwood, and in August Kirkwood made him colonel of the newly formed Thirty-Second Iowa Infantry.[5]

Surgeon Thomas O. Edwards also refused to serve under Williams again and he, too, submitted his resignation. Edwards had become involved in his own problems as well as his ongoing conflict with Assistant Surgeon Daniel Cool. He left the army and did not return.[6]

General Benjamin Prentiss, Major William Stone, and the other Shiloh captives were sent south as prisoners of war, first to Montgomery, Alabama, then to Macon, Georgia, then to Selma, Alabama.

The war was now in its second year and thousands of soldiers were held as prisoners by both sides. It was obvious that some sort of prisoner exchange system was needed. In June both the Union and the Confederacy agreed to send representatives to Washington D.C. to arrange terms for an equitable system.

Both sides agreed to release some prisoners to help in the negotiations. General Prentiss selected William Stone to represent the Union officers captured at Shiloh. Stone received a forty-day parole, was released from prison, and sent to Washington. However, the conference was not immediately successful and an exchange system was not agreed upon. William Stone blamed Secretary of War Simon Cameron and President Lincoln for giving into Cameron on the issue. Stone made his position clear in a letter to the *Dubuque Daily Times.*

> Nearly every member of congress and a majority of the cabinet are strongly committed in favor of a speedy and general exchange. The President, too is known to favor it, but for the present, refers the question to the Secretary of War, who, for reasons which I am unable to comprehend, thinks it would be inexpedient, at this particular juncture, to give the rebels 15,000 men and receive the same number in return. To our limited comprehension the policy adopted by the War Department, for the prosecution of the war, may not be apparent, yet it is our duty as soldiers to believe that everything they do is for the best, and submit to their action without question or complaint.[7]

While in Washington Major Stone did everything he could for those he had left behind. He went to the paymaster general and, on his own guarantee, obtained $15,000 in back pay for his men. He sent half of the money home to their families and used the other half to purchase clothing for the prisoners (which the Confederates allowed them to receive).

When the negotiations fell through, Major Stone was on the thirty-eighth day of his parole. If he could not be part of an agreed upon exchange, he had to return to prison. As he said in his letter:

We have failed to secure the consent of our Government to a general exchange of prisoners, as proposed by the rebel authorities. This determines the necessity of our return to the South to remain in close confinement, it may be, till the termination of the war....

This is my last hour in Washington. I am anxious to return to Dixie, where my rations of corn await me.[8]

Stone was a free man in Washington. He could have ignored his parole but he didn't. He traveled south under a flag of truce, crossed into Virginia, surrendered to Confederate authorities, and was taken to the infamous Libby Prison in Richmond, Virginia. Jefferson Davis, president of the Confederacy, was kept informed of the negotiations. When he heard that Major Stone had gallantly chosen to surrender himself, Davis immediately ordered that the major be released. President Davis extended Stone's parole by 15 days and sent him back to renew the negotiations. The conference was reconvened, and this time it was successful. An exchange system instituted for that fall served reasonably well for over a year. Major Stone did not have to return to prison, and Prentiss and the other Shiloh captives were exchanged between August and December 1862.[9]

Stone's activities as a prisoner/diplomat made him famous across Iowa. He returned home to Knoxville for a rest and resigned his commission in the Third Iowa Infantry. Governor Kirkwood immediately rewarded him with a promotion to colonel and gave him command of the Twenty-Second Iowa Infantry.[10]

Matthew Trumbull was granted a furlough to return home and heal. On his way home, Trumbull visited friends in Dubuque. One wrote: "I have just seen Capt. M. M. Trumbull, Co. I, 3d Iowa. He was wounded in the thigh, and looks emaciated and care-worn from his recent sufferings."[11] Another friend said, "He looks very thin, though he seems in good spirits and says he is improving rapidly."[12]

On 29 June, while Trumbull was home in Clarksville, Governor Kirkwood received this petition signed by ten captains and lieutenants of the Third Iowa Infantry.

Sir:

The resignation of Lieutenant Colonel John Scott makes it necessary to fill the position occupied by him by your appointment. Learning that in such cases you desire views of the officers of the line, we most respectfully ask your excellency to appoint Capt. M. M. Trumbull to the position of Lieutenant Colonel of this regiment.

We most cordially endorse him as a brave and efficient officer who has the confidence of his comrades in arms to a remarkable degree.[13]

The governor let it be known, unofficially, that Trumbull would probably get the promotion, but he did nothing immediately.

While both Trumbull and Colonel Williams were home on furlough, the Third Iowa helped pursue the Confederate army from Corinth, Mississippi, to central Tennessee. Corinth, once the great Confederate staging ground, became an important Union supply base. In mid-June Colonel Williams came back from his furlough and took command of the regiment. He had outlasted most of his old enemies but there were still bad feelings. S. D. Thompson wrote: "Colonel Williams resumed command of the regiment and began…to renew his obnoxious practices." (Williams had demoted a sergeant and placed the quartermaster under arrest.)[14]

Trumbull was still home in Clarksville when trouble with Colonel Williams began. Trumbull was one of many officers who overstayed their furloughs without having gone through the correct procedures for extensions. This caused a great deal of difficulty for the army as it tried to reorganize after the Shiloh battle. General William Sherman, now second in command, issued orders that all such officers return to duty or be subject to arrest.

Colonel Williams obeyed General Sherman and brought charges of desertion against Trumbull and other officers. Trumbull was furious and responded on 17 July by sending Williams a letter of resignation.

> Sir:
> I herewith tender my resignation as Captain in the 3rd Iowa Infantry. My reasons are 1st. My health is not in a condition to allow me to bear the fatigue of active duty.
> 2nd. Sickness in my family. My wife has been for some time past, and is now, in so delicate a state of health, as to render her quite unable to conduct the management of a large family without my assistance.
> 3rd. The harmony of the regiment may be promoted by my retirement.[15]

Colonel Williams refused to accept Trumbull's resignation. Williams made it clear that the charges were not his doing; he had only obeyed General Sherman. The charges against Trumbull were withdrawn and so was his resignation.

Over the next few months, friction between Trumbull and Williams was kept to a minimum because of Williams's poor health. He had never fully recovered from his Shiloh injuries and suffered from severe bronchitis and dysentery. He spent much of the summer and early fall of 1862 on leave while Trumbull did the command duties. In September Williams finally admitted that he was in no shape to continue trying to lead the regiment. In spite of the fact that Governor Kirkwood had not made the promotion official, Colonel Williams ordered Trumbull to wear the insignia of a lieutenant colonel and take command of the regiment. S. D. Thompson wrote:

> He accordingly put on the uniform of Lt. Colonel, and we began to address him by his new title, rejoiced that, at a time when an encounter with the enemy seemed probable, we were led by an officer of such gallantry and merit.[16]

Lieutenant Thompson was pleased with Trumbull's command style.

> Our duty was heavy; but Col. Trumbull endeavored to lighten it as much as possible. Our foraging expeditions furnished some excitement, and, notwithstanding very stringent orders against plundering, generally kept us supplied with fresh vegetables and meat. Col. Trumbull was an excellent drill master, and under him our regiment improved rapidly in the evolutions of the battalion.[16]

(Governor Kirkwood saw to it that Trumbull's actual commission as lieutenant colonel was back-dated to 10 August 1862.)

In the fall of 1862, Southern slavery was still a legal institution. But where the Yankee armies marched, thousands of slaves fled their masters and followed. General William Sherman tried to stem the tide of black refugees by forbidding his men to encourage slaves to leave their homes. General Halleck, however, addressed the issue by giving orders that authorized Union regiments to employ blacks as cooks, laborers, and teamsters.

Halleck was following the example of General Benjamin Butler who claimed that as Confederate soldiers defended trenches that slaves had dug and ate rations grown and transported by slaves, the slaves were legitimate objects of military confiscation, no different than horses or wagons. Butler applied the name of contraband to the slaves. Other high-ranking Union officers, such as John C. Frémont, used the contraband argument to free slaves.

Colonel Nelson Williams ignored General Sherman, embraced Halleck's orders, and welcomed the runaways. Lieutenant S. D. Thompson said that:

> Contrabands thronged the camps in large numbers, and soon became an important element in the *material* of the army. All that came within our lines were received and put to work, and supplied with clothing and subsistence. This policy was viewed by the soldiers with very general approbation.[18]

Years later, when Trumbull was a writer living in Chicago, he told this story of the army and the escaped slaves.

> In 1862 the regiment that I belonged to was marching through Tennessee, and every night when we went into camp a lot of negroes had to be provided for, who had left the plantations to follow the flag of liberty. Our colonel distributed those negroes among the different companies as servants—so many to each mess. One evening he noticed a disturbance in the camp and inquired the cause of it. "Why," said a disputant, "our mess ain't got its full ration of nigger."[19]

When Trumbull took command of the regiment in September, he continued to welcome the escapees, but there was no hard and fast rule concerning the situation.

General Sherman generally sided with slave owners who wanted their property back, which put him into conflict with officers who wanted them freed. Trumbull made his position very clear—no escaped slave who entered his camp would be returned to bondage. Ray Boston, in "Respectable Radical," quoted an old friend of Trumbull's who told this story (though Trumbull was not a general at the time).

> One day, from headquarters, he spied an excitement in camp. Hurrying to the scene, he learned that a slave-holder wished to reclaim his slave, a Negro girl, dressed in men's clothes, engaged in the camp cooking for a mess of union soldiers. The general, discovering the cause of the trouble, ordered the slave-holder to leave the camp, refusing to surrender the colored girl. The next day the slave-holder returned with an order from General Sherman asking Trumbull to surrender the slave. After reading the order he tore it into strips, exclaiming: "I don't care about the orders of General Sherman; get out of this camp—*git, git, git.*" And he got.[20]

In another case when he refused to surrender a slave, Trumbull explained why he refused to use the contraband legalism as a defense.

> The slaves were not confiscated; they were freed. It is true that Gen. Butler in the early part of the war did confiscate some slaves under the prevarication that they were, "contraband of war," a mischievous pretense, which proved to be a sophism both in ethics and politics. About the same time I had the honor to emancipate a slave who had taken refuge in my camp. I did it on grounds in opposite to those claimed by Gen. Butler. I refused to give the Negro up, not because he was a chattel forfeited, but because he was a man, and therefore impossible to be a contraband of war.[21]

As the war continued during the fall of 1862, Corinth was the most important Union stronghold in Mississippi. If the Confederacy was ever to win the state back, Corinth must be recaptured. On 3 October 1862, a Confederate army under General Earl Van Dorn numbering 22,000 men advanced on Corinth. A Union army of roughly equal numbers defended the city under General William Rosecrans. When U.S. Grant discovered the Confederate attack on Corinth, he hurried as many reinforcements as possible to Rosecrans.

Grant's reinforcements were not needed. In a two-day battle, Rosecrans successfully defended the city. The reinforcements arrived in time to help Rosecrans pursue Van Dorn's army. The Confederates marched to the southwest of town and tried to get across the Hatchie River at the Davis Bridge before the Union troops caught up. If Van Dorn was able cross the river and burn the bridge, he might save his army. If he didn't get across the bridge in time, he could be trapped against the river.

Worse for Van Dorn, and unknown to him, was that Grant had also ordered Stephen Hurlbut's Fourth Division to march from Bolivar, Tennessee, to Corinth. The line of march brought Hurlbut's division to the Hatchie River on the west side of the Davis Bridge. Van Dorn was trapped between two Union armies, and the bridge was the critical point.

Van Dorn sent his cavalry ahead to secure the bridge, which it did. Then he sent the first of his infantry columns across. On the west side of the river lay the road west to Tennessee through a pass in a line of hills known as Matamora Heights. On that road, Hurlbut hurried his First and Second brigades forward, secured the pass, and formed his lead regiments into battle line. (Trumbull and the Third Iowa were in reserve as part of the division's Third Brigade and watched the first regiments deploy from Matamora Heights.)

The Confederate infantry stopped just as it was crossing the bridge and marching into a trap. The first Confederates to cross formed a line and tried to hold back Hurlbut's troops long enough to get the rest of the army across the bridge and up to the hills on the other side. The rest of Van Dorn's infantry stayed on the high ground beyond the river and dug in, bringing their artillery to the front where it could rake anything trying to cross the bridge.

But the Confederates didn't reckon on Stephen Hurlbut, a leader who could inspire men. Hurlbut was a Southern born Yankee, a veteran of a South Carolina militia unit and the Seminole wars, and he never lost his military bearing. That day he stood before his men wearing his best uniform and riding his favorite horse. He led the first running column across the bridge and captured it before the Confederates could set it on fire. The Third Iowa and the rest of the reserves hurried forward to be ready if needed. Confederate infantry fought back fiercely. Sergeant George L. Wright of "A" Company Third Iowa, described watching Hurlbut's lead brigade capture the bridge.

> The contest was fierce, parties came in close contact, charges desperate and deadly were everywhere made, Generals, Aid de Camps and orderlies flew to and fro in hot haste with orders and cheering words…a grand effort was made, and the opposing force was compelled to yield and the bridge was carried and in our possession.[22]

Capturing the bridge was just the start. Hurlbut's men then pressed forward over a narrow road to a small plain and up the high ridge where Van Dorn's men were massed. Both infantry and cannon fired down at the Yankees. Hurlbut rallied his men and tried to get them to charge up the slope, but the rebel fire was too heavy. The men were trapped below the ridge. If they retreated across the bridge, they would be cut to pieces. The men crowded together on the road and plain. They took what cover they could and fired back up at the rebels. With Hurlbut's lead brigade trapped below the ridge, the Confederate guns concentrated on them and ceased firing at the bridge. Retreating men helping wounded comrades took advantage of the momentary reprieve and hurried across the bridge back to Matamora Heights. They were joined by troops escorting rebel prisoners and skulkers fleeing the fight. General Hurlbut took the moment to gallop back across the bridge under some gunfire from rebel marksmen trained to spot officers and their staffs. He got to the other side, rode straight to Trumbull and the other Third Brigade officers, and told them to get their men ready to go in.

Trumbull formed his men into marching column and ordered them to fix bayonets. With their muskets at the right shoulder-shift position—the running position—Trumbull's Third Iowa was ready. Hurlbut placed himself at the front of the brigade. A Third Iowa soldier, writing under the name St. Charles, described Hurlbut as being "…as cool as upon review." Trumbull rode at the head of his Third Iowa boys.[23]

Confederate gunners on the ridge saw the reinforcements forming and cut loose with everything they had while their infantry joined in. It looked as if no one would live if he tried to cross the bridge. Two soldiers were reported to be so terrified that, in full view of their comrades, they put their hands over the muzzles of their muskets and fired, mangling their hands rather than face the bridge. Hurlbut and Trumbull ignored the deadly fire that swept the bridge and crashed into the buildings on either side. They sat straight in their saddles, drew their swords, and took their men across. Private "St. Charles" wrote: "Capt. Trumbull led us into the fight and a better specimen of bravery was never seen."[24]

Trumbull led over three hundred men across the bridge, galloping his horse, his men running close behind. Almost sixty of them were hit by exploding shells and musket fire. Once across, Trumbull and his men became entangled in the crowd on the road and plain below the ridge. Rebel gunfire still poured down at them, and Trumbull's men were becoming lost in the death, smoke, noise, and confusion. Trumbull looked up at the ridge where he expected the rebels to take advantage of the chaos and sweep down on them. He then looked back to the bridge and found himself cheering. General Hurlbut, in another heroic moment, had ridden back across the bridge and was now leading more reinforcements across. Seeing Hurlbut mounted on his big horse at the head of a fresh Union column, Trumbull took heart. He ordered his color bearer to plant the flag close by so the men could see it. He stood up in his stirrups, raised his sword, and shouted, "Men of the Third Iowa, will you stand by me this day?" The men cheered! Trumbull waved his sword again and yelled, "Then here's a man that never retreats this day!"

S. D. Thompson put it well: "Could we have asked for a better leader?"[25]

As Hurlbut thundered across the bridge, Trumbull raised his sword, spurred his mount, and led the Iowa troops forward, up the steep hill, and into the enemy trenches. All three brigades charged with Trumbull, fighting hand to hand for every inch of ground. By 4 o'clock the rebels abandoned their fortifications on the hill and retreated. As they fled the field, Hurlbut and Trumbull pushed their men forward, trying to force Van Dorn's troops back on Rosecrans' army that was coming from Corinth.

But there was no Union army on the horizon. Rosecrans was too late. Van Dorn's army found another bridge across the Hatchie and escaped. Hurlbut's victory at the Davis Bridge should have been a glorious triumph, but instead, it goes down in history as nothing more than a large-scale skirmish at the tail end of the Battle of Corinth.

For the Third Iowa infantry, two men were killed and sixty wounded in the Hatchie battle. Eight of the wounded soldiers were from Trumbull's Butler County Union Guards.[26]

That night Trumbull bivouacked his men on the field, kept them in battle line, and sent out patrols to retrieve the wounded. Over the next two days, the men buried the dead, cared for the wounded, and collected the abandoned rebel weapons. When the men finally returned to their camps, they were exhausted, hungry, and proud. Trumbull assembled the men and took a few minutes to thank them for their courage and obedience to orders. He told them that General Hurlbut had personally witnessed them in the battle and had praised them. Trumbull ended his speech by calling for three cheers for Hurlbut and the other generals. The men responded heartily. When they finished cheering the generals, the men spontaneously raised three successive cheers for Trumbull.[27]

Trumbull wrote the official Report of the Battle of the Hatchie.

> I have the honor to report the part taken by the 3rd Iowa Infantry in the battle of the 5th of October. The 3rd Iowa, 300 strong, was on the right of the 1st Brigade (Gen. Lauman) and formed part of the reserve. When the reserve was ordered into action, the 3rd Iowa led, crossing the river with a cheer, and at a double quick, under so severe a fire that fifty-seven men were shot down in a few minutes including over half the commissioned officers present. This necessarily threw the regiment into some confusion especially as the road was very narrow and encumbered with a good deal of underbrush, and the men pressing forward got intermixed with the men of other regiments. I saw no way to extricate the regiment but by planting the colors in the middle of the road and ordering the men to rally to them and form a new line of battle. This was promptly done, nearly every man springing to his place. The regiment then moved forward up the hill, in company with other regiments which had adopted the same plan, the enemy retreating as we advanced....
>
> The conduct of the rank and file in crossing the bridge, under the terrible fire of the enemy batteries, and in rallying to the flag as promptly as they did, deserves the highest praise.
>
> Several cases of individual bravery among the men, I shall bring to the notice of the General commanding the Brigade, as soon as I have investigated the cir-

cumstances....I am ashamed to say that, a few, a very few cases of misconduct in the presence of the enemy, have been reported to me, which on further investigation, I shall submit to the General commanding the Brigade with a request that they be submitted to a general court martial.

I have the honor to be, sir, with great respect, your obedient servant,
M. M. Trumbull,
Captain, Commanding Third Iowa Infantry [28]

CHAPTER 10

Tattoo

Victory at the Hatchie was credited to General Hurlbut who had formulated the battle plan and personally led his troops in the execution of that plan. His heroism was an inspiration for officers such as Matthew Trumbull and the rest of the soldiers under his command. As a reward, Hurlbut was promoted to major general which meant a new assignment. The Fourth Division was called out in a grand review to say farewell to Hurlbut. Lieutenant S. D. Thompson described the ceremony.

> As the thinned battalions marched past him, their battered flags saluting, with so many brave, familiar faces absent, the General gazed upon his men, and the men turned their eyes toward their general, with an affection which it does not seem possible could have grown up between soldier and commander in the short space of seven months.[1]

When Hurlbut turned the division over to its new commander, he issued a special order—a farewell tribute to his officers and troops. It opened with these words:

> Comrades in battle, partakers of the weary march and the long watches! By your discipline and courage the victory has been won, and the title of the "Fighting Fourth," earned at Shiloh, has been burnished with additional splendor on the Hatchie.[2]

Matthew Trumbull had won as much glory on the Hatchie as anyone, but as was true of so many Civil War soldiers, he went into the battle a very sick man. His Shiloh wounds were not fully healed and he also suffered from bronchitis. Trumbull managed to pull himself together for the Hatchie campaign, but after the battle he was sent to the military hospital at Corinth. In early November he recovered enough to rejoin the regiment at La Grange, Tennessee.

Colonel Nelson G. Williams, a man as sick as Trumbull, also returned to the regiment at its La Grange camp. Williams took command, and the old feud began immediately. Colonel Williams did not see Trumbull as anything but a threat, an ally of John Scott, a rival for rank. And Trumbull could not accept Williams's roughshod ways. He, not Williams, was the more experienced officer. Williams was late at Monroe Station, retreated at Shelbina, missed the Blue Mills battle, was knocked out of the Shiloh fight early, and was too sick to fight at the Hatchie. Any of the regiment's battle glory was won under Scott, Stone, and Trumbull—not Nelson Williams. It was no surprise that on 17 November 1862, Trumbull submitted a letter of resignation to the regiment's adjutant, Lieutenant G. W. Cushman. (The former adjutant, Fitzroy Sessions, resigned in October due to poor health.)

> I hereby respectfully tender my resignation as Lieut. Col., 3d Iowa Infty. My reasons are, I have been in active service in the field for about 17 months, during the latter half of which time I have been in very poor health. Last winter I suffered from a very severe bronchial infection, and have never been thoroughly well since. For the past two months I have been troubled with a severe and constant pain in the chest, which renders me quite unable to endure the exposures incident to camp life. I am also suffering from an injury received at Shiloh, which renders walking or riding very painful and difficult.[3]

The regiment's new surgeon, Benjamin F. Keables, endorsed the letter. Keables replaced Daniel M. Cool who resigned in September. Keables declared that due to his health, Trumbull was "…rendered useless to the government." The resignation was accepted and endorsed by General U. S. Grant, who was back in command of the Army of the Tennessee, effective on 24 November 1862.[4]

Lieutenant Thompson wrote that Trumbull, "…tendered his resignation for reasons which were well understood and appreciated by his friends."[5]

When the news that Trumbull's resignation was accepted reached the Third Iowa camp at La Grange, the officers of the regiment threw a celebration in honor of the Hero of the Hatchie. A list of resolutions was adopted by every man present.

> Resolved: That while in command of this Regiment Col. M. M. Trumbull has given universal satisfaction to the officers and men under him.
> Resolved: That by the resignation of Colonel Trumbull our regiment has lost a popular and efficient officer, his brother officers a sociable and generous companion, and the government one of its coolest and bravest soldiers.
> Resolved: That we deeply regret the circumstances that has forced him to resign, and our sincere wishes for the speedy recovery of his health accompany him in his retirement.
> Resolved: That Col. Trumbull by his coolness and bravery at the battles of Blue Mills, Shiloh, and the Hatchie, has made a record that is equaled by few and surpassed by none and should last while coolness is approved and bravery commended.
> Resolved: That these resolutions express the sentiment of the entire regiment, both officers and men, to the best of our knowledge.[6]

Trumbull took the floor and, with tears in his eyes, responded:

I am overpowered by the generous expression of confidence, friendship and sympathy contained in the resolutions read to me. I cannot express my emotions of regret at the circumstances which compelled me to retire from the service. I am thankful to you for these kindly expressions, but am still more thankful for the ready obedience and the warm personal regard you have given me during the time I have been in command of the Third Iowa Infantry. It has been my singular good fortune that while I have always insisted on the observance of the strictest discipline, I have never heard a murmur or an unkind remark from any officer under my command, and the noble and patriotic devotion with which you have followed me into battle, compels a lifelong gratitude.

I will consider it a personal favor if you will convey the sentiments expressed towards yourselves to the noble fellows in your command; the rank and file of the regiment, the honored heroes of this war. They have clung to me with the affectionate devotion of children to a parent: assure them that I reciprocate their feelings. At the bloody bridge on the Hatchie they said that they would follow me anywhere that I would lead them, and they did, into the jaws of death and gates of hell.[7]

Two days later the regiment received orders to march and, for the first time, Trumbull was not with them. S. D. Thompson wrote, "We marched at six o'clock. Colonel Trumbull stood before his tent as we started. The tears came into the gallant Colonel's eyes as he looked at the boys for the last time."[8]

In his book *Reflections With the Third Iowa*, Lieutenant Thompson added this footnote concerning Trumbull:

He was with us in all our battles, and on all occasions behaved with a degree of courage and resolution seldom equaled, nowhere surpassed....His generosity knew no distinction of rank; for a gallant officer or soldier he could not do too much, and there was but one offense which he could not forgive: misbehavior in the face of the enemy. To those guilty parties he was particularly intolerant. In short, he possessed in a high degree the elements which make up a successful soldier....[9]

Two weeks after Trumbull left the regiment, Colonel Williams also resigned citing "continued ill health."[10] Williams's resignation was also accepted.

Colonel Nelson G. Williams went home to his Delaware County farm. Although Governor Kirkwood submitted Williams's name for promotion to brigadier general, an officer with Williams's record had no chance of being confirmed by the U.S. Senate. Williams's part in the Civil War was finished. He was a successful man who could have stayed home, but he stepped forward and became another Iowa volunteer damaged by the war. Williams was remembered in Captain A. A. Stuart's important book titled *Iowa Colonels and Regiments*, a history of Iowa Civil War colonels, published in 1865. Stuart, of the Seventeenth Iowa Infantry, met Williams once, shortly before the colonel resigned.

> ...his person and manners impressed me so strongly that I am still able to recall them. He has a dark complexion, dark eyes, a large head, and a rather low and retreating forehead. In person, he is short, and heavy set, with full chest and large, square shoulders. He is not attractive in his personal appearance.
>
> While sitting by himself, he looked grum and uncompanionable; but his whole manner changed as soon as he was addressed. I saw that he was fond of amusement, and all its concomitants: indeed, there have been few officers who would not occasionally indulge in a game of cards, *et cetera*.
>
> As a commanding officer, I judged him to be precise and exacting; and I have since learned that this was his character. While in command of his regiment, he was tyrannical, and by a majority of both officers and men, sincerely hated.[11]

When the officers of the regiment were informed of Williams's resignation, they circulated a petition that most of the regiment's captains and lieutenants signed calling on Governor Kirkwood to recall Trumbull. Captain Aaron Brown of "F" Company, the next in line to command the Third Iowa, explained their reasons in a letter to Governor Kirkwood.

> Dear Sir—
>
> Herewith enclosed is a petition from officers of this regt. asking for the appointment of Lt. Col. M. M. Trumbull as Colonel, to fill the vacancy occasioned by the resignation of Col. Williams—The request has my most hearty approval. Trumbull has been tried often but was never found wanting—he possesses the requisites for a good commander in a high degree and has the most unbounded confidence of both officers and men. His return to the regt. in the capacity of Colonel would be hailed with gladness by a very large majority.[12]

Sergeant George L. Wright of "A" Company wrote a letter to the *Dubuque Daily Times* that said:

> A petition by the staff and line officers for the return of M. M. Trumbull, as our colonel, has been sent to his excellency, Governor Kirkwood. Perhaps the ranks ought not to say anything, but they are the future party power, and to his excellency they too would cry "Send us Trumbull! He has successfully led us upon the bloody battlefield; we know he is brave and we can trust him."[13]

Governor Kirkwood ignored the petition. Captain Aaron Brown was advanced to colonel, giving him the distinction of being the only Iowa colonel in the Civil War to have been born in Mississippi.

Matthew Trumbull returned to his wife and sons in Clarksville. He needed time to rest and heal, but he did not consider himself out of the war. Trumbull expected to do just what John Scott and William Stone had done—use his service in the Third Iowa as a means of advancement. He could not have known that he was riding into tragedy and military obscurity.

CHAPTER 11

The Ninth Iowa Cavalry

If Matthew Trumbull had dreams of domestic tranquility in Clarksville, they were unfulfilled. The war had produced another casualty—his marriage. Christiana's story was the story of a Civil War wife. She married a glory hunter who marched off on his abolitionist crusade while she stayed home in Clarksville with four very young sons (Matthew Jr., the oldest, was twelve in 1862). Her health weakened under the strain.

Matthew Trumbull, in the courteous fashion of the age, did not write of his marriage. However, sometime after the Hatchie battle, he and Christiana divorced. What happened to Christiana is not known. Trumbull raised their four sons who grew up to be a gold prospector, a railroad engineer, a store clerk, and a business secretary.[1]

Trumbull left Clarksville in December 1862. He moved to Cedar Falls and opened a law office. His business card read: "Will attend promptly in the collection of soldiers' back pay and bounty." His old friend, Henry Perkins, editor of the *Cedar Falls Gazette,* welcomed him with these words:

> If Lieut. Col. Trumbull can conduct a case through the labyrinthian intricacies of the law as successfully as he can lead a body of men upon an enemy's stronghold, he will rank A No. 1 in his profession.[2]

Life in Cedar Falls went well for Trumbull. He had a thriving law practice, was often asked to lecture to local civic organizations, and had old comrades nearby. Former adjutant Fitzroy Sessions moved back to Cedar Falls in the fall of 1862. Lieutenant John Wayne of the Pioneer Greys, who was wounded and captured at Shiloh, resigned and came back home after a prisoner exchange in December 1862.

Cedar Falls was a solid Republican town that firmly supported the war. However, a small but equally solid Democratic anti-war element existed in town. Twice anti-war editors tried to publish Democratic newspapers to rival Perkins' *Gazette* but found few readers and fewer advertisers. Cedar Falls Democrats kept in close contact with Dennis Mahoney's Dubuque Democrats, and, on occasion, there was trouble. When Stilson Hutchins, Mahoney's co-editor of the *Dubuque Herald,* visited Cedar Falls, Fitzroy Sessions confronted him at the Carter House Hotel and beat him bloody with his fists. When John Hodnett of the *Dubuque Herald* visited, a team of vigilantes met him and chased him out of town.[3]

In February 1863 the *Dubuque Daily Times* ran this short piece.

> The Knights of the Golden Circle have so stimulated the members of their fraternity that in Waverly, Cedar Falls and other places in the Cedar Valley, they are heard shouting in the streets for "Jeff Davis and the Southern Confederacy." An instance of the kind occurred in Cedar Falls last week, in the hearing of Colonel M. M. Trumbull, late of the Iowa 3rd, when that gentleman immediately went for his revolver, declaring that he would shoot the scoundrel. While he was gone, the Secesh gathered in large numbers on one side and the Republicans began to collect on the other. At first a fight seemed inevitable, but the crowd finally dispersed, and there was no blood shed.[4]

The Cedar Falls home and law practice did not mean that Trumbull had surrendered his aspirations to military rank and glory. Rest and life in Iowa had restored his health and in mid-December 1862 he took another military physical and was declared fit for duty. He wrote to Governor Kirkwood and declared that he was ready to be recommissioned.[5]

Trumbull's willingness to go back into the army was not matched by Governor Kirkwood's willingness to give him a new command. Trumbull waited throughout the winter and spring of 1863. In June 1863 Assistant Adjutant General P. E. Hall resigned and Governor Kirkwood appointed Trumbull in his place. This was an important bureaucratic position that allowed Trumbull to travel across the state, but it was not the field command he wanted.

Trumbull served under Adjutant General Nathaniel Bradley Baker. Baker, a former governor of New Hampshire, was a hard drinking Democrat, qualities that did not impress Trumbull. The two clashed on occasion but Trumbull and Baker managed to work together for the next few months. Baker ran the Adjutant General's office out of Davenport, and Trumbull was forced to divide his time between there and Cedar Falls.

Iowa's anti-war movement was strongest in southern Iowa, almost an extension of Missouri. In August 1863 there was an explosion of violence in Keokuk County. A so-called army of pro-Confederate Iowans under the leadership of a Tennessee-born Baptist minister named George Cyphert Tally, invaded the town of South English. Tally led the way standing in the bed of a wagon, a pistol in one hand and a Bowie knife in the other. The Tally army was met by armed Republicans, shots were fired, Tally fell dead, and one of his men was wounded. Tally's men retreated, but vowed to return.

Two days later, after Tally had been buried, hundreds of his supporters from Keokuk, Wapello, Mahaska, and Poweshiek counties gathered near the Skunk River and prepared to march on the towns of South English and Sigourney and avenge their leader. Frightened citizens sent envoys to meet with Governor Kirkwood, who was in Davenport at the time, and ask for protection. Kirkwood acted swiftly, promising to call out the Iowa militia and to come to Sigourney in person.

Adjutant General Baker had organized militia companies in every county in the state, the forerunner of the present day Iowa National Guard, one of Baker's greatest legacies. Kirkwood had only to call them into action. Adjutant Baker was not in Iowa, his father had died and Baker was in New Hampshire attending to family, so the duties of Adjutant General fell to Matthew Trumbull.

Trumbull, working closely with Governor Kirkwood, called eleven companies of militia into service and ordered them to occupy the towns of Sigourney and South English. Trumbull, with his experience in Missouri, knew the difficulties of trying to occupy a divided land, gave strict orders to the militia captains:

> The soldiers will avoid all occasion of quarrel with the citizens, and are hereby strictly enjoined not to injure or molest any citizen, either in person or property, unless in execution of orders and in the line of duty.
>
> The military force at this place will be strictly subordinate to the civil authority, and will be under the direction of the sheriff. They are only to protect and assist the officers of the law in the performance of their duties. [6]

Governor Kirkwood and Assistant Adjutant Trumbull traveled by train to Sigourney, hours ahead of the troops, arriving after nightfall. They found a divided, tension-filled town. Soldiers of a Sigourney militia company patrolled the streets but half the company did not have arms, and every street corner was lit by torches and seemed to have a crowd of pro-Tally speech makers. Kirkwood and Trumbull were driven directly from the train station to the court house where a mob was gathered, many of the Tally men shouted curses at the Governor and his general as they stepped from the carriage. Kirkwood was at his furious best. He refused to be intimidated and backed only by Trumbull, he stood on the court house steps and gave one of his best speeches. He shouted down the noisy crowd, saying that troops were on the way and, "that he didn't propose to have any fire-in-the-rear rebellion in Iowa, and unless they dispersed before morning he would have them shot down like dogs."[7] The crowd dispersed and Kirkwood and Trumbull waited throughout the night but there was no violence from the Tally men.

The next morning the first militia company arrived from Muscatine, and during the day others came from Washington and Mount Pleasant. The troops crowded the town, and, ignoring Trumbull's order, trashed the office and smashed the press of the local Democratic newspaper. They arrested some of the Tally men who had remained in town and then prepared to go after the Tally army. But there was no army left, the men had gone home, the "Tally War," or "Skunk River War" was over.

Two great turning points in the war came on the national 4th of July holiday, making 1863 a critical year. In the East, the Army of Northern Virginia, under General Robert E. Lee, began its miserable retreat from the blood-soaked fields and hills of Gettysburg, Pennsylvania. In the West, General U. S. Grant formally accepted the surrender of the city of Vicksburg, Mississippi, and of the army that had defended the city.

Trumbull and the rest of the people of the Cedar Valley watched Grant's Vicksburg campaign carefully, for everyone had a son or a friend in those ranks. Vicksburg was the last Confederate stronghold on the Mississippi River. When it fell, the Confederacy was split in two, and the river became one more Union highway. From the fall of 1862 to the summer of 1863, Grant had maneuvered and fought his way to the city. His winter campaigns were muddy, rain-soaked horrors with thousands dying of disease in the wet camps. His battles were bloody charges into massed rebel gunfire that often seemed to have no purpose except slaughter. Grant's campaign finally succeeded when a siege starved the rebels out.

When Vicksburg fell, every town in the Cedar Valley exploded with patriotic joy and celebration, but the enthusiasm was ruined by the terrible news of 12 July.

Throughout the Vicksburg campaign, Confederate General Joseph E. Johnston commanded an army that hovered near Vicksburg, threatening to relieve the city from the rear. But Johnston never came to Vicksburg's rescue and, after the city fell, Grant sent the Fourth Division against Johnston at Jackson, Mississippi. Joseph E. Johnston was a defensive fighter, a master of entrenchments, always eager to force the enemy to charge into his musket fire. Johnston's army was well dug in at Jackson, but the Union forces attacked anyway. Confederates forced the Yankees to fall back and prepare to make a second assault. The First Brigade (still commanded by Colonel Isaac C. Pugh) was left in an extreme advance position with no support on either flank. When they received orders to attack, Colonel Pugh could not believe it and asked for clarification. But there was no mistake—the brigade was to attack alone. The attack was made on Johnston's army and the First Brigade was chopped to pieces.

The Third Iowa Infantry went into the battle with two hundred and twenty-three men, and fifteen officers. One hundred and fourteen of them were shot in a matter of moments. Colonel Aaron Brown led the Third and went down with a rebel minie ball in the thigh. The Butler County Union Guards suffered terribly—seven were killed, six wounded, six were taken captive, and three were missing.[8]

Trumbull chaffed at being out of the war. He was fit, experienced, and ready, but the governor could not seem to find a command for him. Trumbull pushed hard to be appointed colonel of the Eighth Iowa Cavalry that was organized in the summer. But that command went to Joseph Dorr. Finally, in August, after the Tally War, Trumbull received permission from Governor Kirkwood to personally raise another cavalry regiment. He was given forty days to get the job done. The Ninth Iowa Cavalry under Trumbull was the last cavalry regiment formed in Iowa during the Civil War.

The *Dubuque Daily Times* ran this announcement:

> Madam Rumor says that Col. Trumbull, the present Assistant Adjutant General of the state, and formerly captain and lieutenant colonel of the 3rd Infantry, is to be the colonel of the new regiment. If this be true, it will not only be no more than an act of justice to a meritorious officer, but will reflect much credit on Governor Kirkwood for making such a selection. The Colonel has not only a first rate military reputation, but his political principles square with the demands of the present hour. He is an Englishman by birth, but his service in the Mexican War and in the present rebellion, have fully proved that the oath which he registered to defend his adopted country has been splendidly redeemed. On assuming command of Co. I, 3d Infantry, over two years ago, he declared that the sword that he drew in the suppression of this rebellion, should never be permanently sheathed until the question of slavery could be discussed with the same freedom and security in the streets of Charleston, South Carolina, as in the city of London....
>
> With such an officer for col. of the Ninth Iowa Cavalry is it a wonder that every volunteer that wishes to remain in such an organization is desirous of getting into this regiment.[9]

While Trumbull sent his recruiters out and campaigned in person to raise his new regiment, Iowa elected a new governor. The Democratic Party put forward General James M. Tuttle in an effort to distance itself from the hard-core anti-war crowd led by Dennis Mahoney. Tuttle was a true Iowa hero. He had led the Second Iowa Infantry over the rebel breastworks at Fort Donelson which made Grant's victory possible.

The Republican Party needed its own war hero and found its man in William M. Stone. Stone was already well-known for his service in the Third Iowa Infantry and for his gallantry as a prisoner/diplomat in Washington. He became more famous for being wounded while bravely leading his Twenty-second Iowa Infantry in battle at Vicksburg. Stone appeared at the nominating convention with his arm still in a sling. He received cheers and well wishes from the assembled delegates. Governor Kirkwood endorsed and actively campaigned for his old friend. Iowa voters chose William Stone over James Tuttle by over thirty thousand votes.[10]

In the meantime, Trumbull found that raising his new regiment presented difficulties. Circumstances were different; the war had changed. In 1861, Trumbull and the other self-titled captains had an exciting time recruiting eager volunteers. But by 1863 the glory and excitement had diminished. The trains that ran through eastern Iowa carried volunteers off to Dixie for two years. Those same trains made countless return trips, carrying those same young men home. Only now they were the wounded returning to recover as best they could, or the dead being brought home for burial. Over half the men Trumbull had recruited in 1861 were brought home on those trains.

The few men left for military service were no longer willing to volunteer for thirteen dollars a month and patriotism. The federal government offered a double incentive: the threat of a draft and a three hundred dollar bounty for a three-year enlistment. State, county, and local payments in both cash and property supplemented the federal bounty payment. Enlistment could be very profitable. "Bounty jumpers" appeared as men who volunteered for one unit, deserted, and volunteered for another unit again and again, getting bounty payments until they were caught. Trumbull's recruiters complained of the lack of recruits, and of Iowa's policy not to offer a state bounty. Because of this, available volunteers left Iowa for better bounties elsewhere. Some recruits to the Ninth Iowa Cavalry turned out to be "bounty jumpers" who were arrested and turned over to their original units.[11]

Yet Trumbull overcame the difficulties. His reputation was solid, and he had friends. One old friend and comrade was John P. Knight, Trumbull's lieutenant who was wounded at Blue Mills while helping Trumbull drag the cannon from the field. Knight was wounded twice more at Shiloh, in the chest and foot, and was left on the field to be captured. He recovered from his wounds while a prisoner of war. After he was exchanged, he returned to the Third with a promotion to captain. When Trumbull called for volunteers, Captain Knight resigned to accept the rank of lieutenant colonel of the Ninth Iowa Cavalry, second in command to Trumbull.[12]

One of Trumbull's best recruiters was his old friend William Haddock, former editor of the *Butler County Jeffersonian*. Haddock sold the paper in late 1861 and raised a company of men that became "E" Company Twelfth Iowa Infantry. (The newspaper continued for another year as the *Butler County Stars and Stripes*.) Haddock and the Twelfth Iowa fought at the Shiloh Hornet's Nest with Prentiss where Haddock was captured and sent south. Once he was exchanged, recovered, and discharged from the Twelfth, he sought a position with Trumbull. Haddock brought thirty volunteers to the Ninth Iowa Cavalry and received the rank of major.[13]

Trumbull's Cedar Falls friend, John Wayne, formerly of "K" Company, Third Iowa (Pioneer Greys), was a veteran of Blue Mills, Shiloh, and the Hatchie. He enlisted as Trumbull's adjutant.[14]

The majority of the men in the ranks were also veteran soldiers. In November Trumbull wrote to Governor Kirkwood:

> My regiment is now full, with a couple of hundred to spare. I am now anxious to get into the field, but I am anxious to go in, in good shape. There is a disposition I think to muster in, in a hurry. We have no assurances at present, as to where our horses, arms, equipment, or anything else, are to come from. If they get us mustered in, we are then, of course, beyond the power of the State authority to help us. So long as the State holds us in hand, we can do something for ourselves.

I think the horses should be purchased in the State. If they get us mustered in they can give us just such horses as they think proper. They can send us into the field, to be equipped there, and my experience shows me, that a regiment in that condition, never gets equipped at all. What I wish you to do…is to keep an eye on the matter, and hold the regiment in hand, until…satisfied that it is well mounted and equipped.

I am jealous for the honor of the State, the Regiment, and myself, that when we get into the field, we should be in position to do something, and gain some credit.[15]

The governor took Trumbull's advice and, as a result, the regiment was well mounted. The officers of the Ninth served on a purchasing board that selected the horses and they "were fine animals." Each squadron was issued horses of the same color so that when the full regiment was on parade it made an impressive appearance.[16]

The regiment was also well trained. The original organization of the Ninth Iowa Cavalry was at Camp Roberts (later Camp Kinsman), one of five military camps at Davenport, Iowa. On 8 December 1863, Trumbull received orders to move the regiment to Benton Barracks, Missouri. The *Davenport News* described the departure.

This splendid regiment of cavalry, Col. Trumbull commanding, were put on board the cars at the depot this morning.…The number of men was 1,115 together with 504 horses and 184,000 pounds of baggage and camp equipage. The men occupied 23 passenger coaches and the horses and baggage 35 freight cars.…This is one of the best regiments that has ever left the state, and in due time will be heard from in the field.[17]

The Ninth Iowa Cavalry arrived at St. Louis on 12 December 1863. However, they were kept in a quarantine camp for a few days due to a few cases of smallpox and then allowed quarters in the barracks. A soldier of the regiment wrote to the *Dubuque Daily Times* and said:

We have all our equipments, horses, ordinance, etc., and all we need is time to drill; when we have gained that I think the 9th will be able to compete with any cavalry regiment that has left Iowa. Too much praise cannot be bestowed on Col. Trumbull and Lt. Col. Knight. They are always on hand, attending to the wants of their men, ever anxious for their comfort; and I am of the opinion that their equals are not in any one regiment in the service. Then we have a model Adjutant, J. Wayne, from Cedar Falls, Iowa. A more obliging and gentlemanly soldier never served his country.[18]

The regiment gained drill time at Benton Barracks, a serious school for soldiers along with nearby Jefferson Barracks. Officers and men were kept under strict military discipline. They were drilled for hours each day, and the officers were required to pass a military board examination before they actually received their commissions. The Ninth stayed at Benton Barracks until well into the spring of 1864 and received far more training than previous cavalry regiments.

Benton Barracks also exposed the Iowa soldiers to a new part of the Union military, black soldiers who were organized into their own regiments and trained along with the other Union soldiers. Trumbull and the other veterans had befriended many black refugees, but the enlistment of black Americans did not begin until after the Emancipation Proclamation of January 1863. By the end of the war, over three hundred thousand Americans of African descent had served as Union soldiers in one hundred and sixty regiments (segregated units under white officers and noncoms).

Many Iowa soldiers served as sergeants and officers in black regiments. Two privates from the Butler County Union Guards served as sergeants in the First Tennessee (Colored) Infantry.[19]

One of the new black regiments was the First Regiment Iowa African Infantry, which later became the Sixtieth U.S. Colored Regiment. The regiment was organized in the summer of 1863 and almost every black man in Iowa of military age served in it. The regiment's only battle was at Wallace's Ferry, Arkansas, July 1864, where eleven of the men were killed in action, three wounded, and no one captured. Three hundred and thirty-two of its soldiers died of disease.[20]

The First Iowa African Infantry was stationed at Benton Barracks at the same time as the Ninth Cavalry, and was presented its regimental flag by the ladies of Keokuk and Muscatine who hand-stitched the flag in honor of the black volunteers. One of Trumbull's men described the men of the regiment: "They were all very large men, hearty and jovial, and presented to me a very unique appearance."[21]

Respect for the black soldiers existed side by side with hatred for them. Men such as Trumbull, who viewed slaves as exploited workers and fellow human beings, served alongside Yankees who looked at blacks as members of an inferior race who deserved to be in a constant state of inferiority to whites. Many whites held blacks responsible for the war and hated them for it. Many others feared that military service would be a black man's claim to full citizenship, something unacceptable to much of America. Racial animosity and violence on the part of Yankee liberators sullied the Northern cause.

In May 1864 Colonel Trumbull received orders to march. He was ready with good officers, disciplined troops, healthy animals, and a strong desire " to do something, and gain some credit."

Trumbull expected to be sent to General Sherman's army that was beginning its famous campaign against Atlanta, Georgia. But Sherman had all the cavalry he needed. Instead garrison troops were needed to police parts of the conquered Confederacy. Trumbull and the Ninth were sent to Arkansas where he was made acting brigadier general and given command of the First Brigade of the Department of the Arkansas, consisting of his own Ninth Iowa Cavalry and both infantry and cavalry regiments from Missouri, Michigan, Illinois, and Arkansas.

One of Trumbull's Arkansas regiments was the Fifty-Seventh U.S. Colored Infantry under Colonel Paul Harwood. The Fifty-Seventh was originally the Fourth Arkansas Infantry-African Descent, a regiment made up of freed Arkansas slaves. (All state regiments of black soldiers were incorporated into the regular army in 1864.)

The army was headquartered at Little Rock and the brigade was headquartered at Devall's Bluffs with Trumbull in command of the post. (Later Trumbull moved his headquarters to Little Rock.)[22]

This was not the duty that Trumbull had sought. In many ways Arkansas was Missouri all over again: a divided state claimed by both sides, controlled by neither, and torn apart by brother against brother feuds. It was a lawless land, filled with bandits, guerrillas, poverty, hatred, and racial tensions. One cause of race hatred was that many former Arkansas slaves joined the Union army and became part of the hated occupation. Over six thousand of the fifteen thousand Union troops in Arkansas were black, and most of them were emancipated slaves.[23]

Trumbull's cavalry was as much a police force as part of an army. Federal troops represented the Union-recognized government and were the only organized force capable of enforcing its laws. It was hard duty. The regiment was seldom together as a unit. Its companies were scattered in different assignments, chasing rebel guerrillas through swamps and rough, hilly scrubland—duty that was wearing on both horses and men.

One guerrilla chieftain, known as Dick Rayburn, became the stuff of campfire legend. Rayburn led a cavalry force of about one hundred men and swooped down on Union stragglers and weakly guarded wagon trains. Captured Union teamsters were stripped of their clothing and valuables, but they were not executed. In true Robin Hood tradition, they were "paroled" and told to go home.

Rayburn, it was said, was a small fellow and so feminine looking that he could easily pass as a woman. In fact, on several occasions he infiltrated Trumbull's camp dressed as a woman. One evening, at a brigade dance (so the story goes), Rayburn even managed to get a dance with one of Trumbull's officers.[24] Many of Rayburn's men were Yankee deserters, but Rayburn did not let just anyone into his outfit. Once when a group of accused thieves from the Ninth Iowa Cavalry deserted and fled to Rayburn he knew that they did not really want to serve the Confederacy. Instead he took them prisoner and turned them back for court martial.[25]

Trumbull's fine regiment and the rest of his brigade began to suffer under the effects of the Arkansas assignment. Sherman and Grant were off on the great campaigns in Georgia and Virginia that would win the war, while Arkansas was a forgotten backwater. There were no glorious battles. The action the regiment saw included one horse killing, man breaking chase, and one scouting expedition after another. Priority for equipment went to Sherman and Grant, not to Arkansas. Keeping the horses fed, shod, and equipped with proper saddles and bridles became almost impossible. Keeping the men fed, uniformed, and equipped was equally difficult.

Trumbull believed that he was a firm disciplinarian, not as harsh as Colonel Williams, but firm. If that was true while he commanded the Third Iowa, it was not true in Arkansas. As troop morale declined, so did military efficiency. On 21 January 1865, the army's Office of Inspector General issued this report on conditions in the Ninth Iowa Cavalry.

> The Ninth Iowa is reported in tolerable condition, but the men look dirty, and the officers allow to much familiarity with the enlisted men. In enforcing discipline the smaller offenses are tried by a field officer's court, but heavier crimes have gone unpunished from the difficulty in getting the offenders before a court martial. In this regiment offenders have escaped punishment who were charged with desertion, sleeping on post, theft, and mutinous conduct.[26]

The charge of mutinous conduct was serious, and conditions only got worse throughout the spring and summer of 1865.

The greatest source of difficulty was the lash-up of the brigade itself, meaning the presence of the Fifty-Seventh U.S. Colored Infantry. Many of the men felt that fighting for the Union and confiscating Confederate "contraband" was one thing, but serving beside black troops was an insult to white men.

When the Fifty-Seventh was first organized, it was expected to be a labor force and not a combat unit. It was issued picks and shovels but not muskets. Colonel Harwood insisted that his men receive proper weapons because they were constantly at the mercy of "Negro haters." As part of Trumbull's brigade, the regiment participated in patrol duty along with the white regiments and was involved in several skirmishes with rebel troops.[27]

The former slaves took full advantage of their freedom. Slaves had been forbidden to learn to read and write but now Union officers in cooperation with black chaplains set up schools for them. An Arkansas newspaper editor wrote this of the men of the Fifty-Seventh:

> Their desire for self improvement is remarkable and notwithstanding the heavy guard and fatigue duties they have had to perform, are making rapid strides toward the attainment of knowledge, and knowledge is power.[28]

In the spring and summer of 1865 Trumbull and his men had to face the fact that they had missed the end of the war. In April, Robert E. Lee surrendered to Grant in Virginia, and Joseph E. Johnston surrendered to William Sherman in North Carolina. Grant and Sherman's armies got to march to Washington D. C. for a two-day

Grand Review of the armies. On 23 May Grant's Army of the Potomac marched down Pennsylvania Avenue to receive a salute from the president. The next day Sherman's army took its turn with its many Iowa regiments, including the last members of the Third Iowa Infantry.

The war was over, and Grant and Sherman's armies seemed to dissolve over night. The soldiers were discharged and sent home. The summer of 1865 was a summer of joyous celebration across Iowa. Every town and city had parades and all-out holidays for the returning soldiers who came back as companies, groups, and individuals throughout the summer.

But in Arkansas, Trumbull and his brigade were not discharged. Their three-year enlistments were not completed, and they were needed as the only law in that part of Arkansas. However, the men did not agree. Iowa's *Roster and Record,* the official history of Iowa troops in the war, said this about the Ninth Iowa Cavalry and postwar Arkansas:

> There was, perhaps, no section of the South where lawlessness and disregard for human life was more prevalent than in the mountainous regions of Arkansas, where roving bands of outlaws were still numerous....Both officers and men felt that it was the duty of the government to increase the strength of the regular army, so that they might be relieved and allowed to return to their homes. While they were given the assurance that this would be done as soon as possible the men were impatient, and a spirit of insubordination was manifested on the part of some of them.[29]

As the war wound down and the army was reorganized, Trumbull was relieved of command of his brigade on 9 June 1865. To acknowledge his months commanding the brigade, Trumbull was promoted to brevet brigadier general. He was transferred to Lewisburg, Arkansas, and took command of the post there. Half the companies of the Ninth Iowa Cavalry were stationed at Lewisburg under Colonel Knight. The other companies were stationed at garrisons nearby. Companies of the Fifty-Seventh Colored Infantry, the Third Arkansas Infantry, and other regiments of Trumbull's former brigade were all encamped near the Lewisburg post.

The men of every regiment in the brigade resented being kept in the army so long after the war was over; they demanded to be released. The "mutinous conduct" reported months earlier only got worse. Men refused to stand guard duty, go out on patrol, or obey orders. In response, Trumbull ordered his officers to crack down on the offenders. Men were forced to wear balls and chains or were punished in other ways. The soldiers' anger was continually fueled by the sense of profound offense at being in the same brigade with black soldiers. On the night of 2 July 1865, all hell broke loose.

By the light of torches and campfires, renegade members of the Ninth Iowa Cavalry and the Third Arkansas Infantry whipped themselves into a killing fury. They stormed out of their camp and attacked the encampment of the Fifty-Seventh Colored. The sentries were rushed and a full scale race riot ensued. It was a Civil War battle only both sides wore Union blue. The white soldiers fired hundreds of shots into the camp, the black soldiers fought back. A private in the Ninth was killed as he rushed a black sentry. Another private from the Third Arkansas was killed and one more wounded.

Officers hurried to inform General Trumbull who quickly gave orders to round up as many reinforcements as could be found. Once the rescue battalion was ready, Trumbull took the lead and galloped to the scene. When he and his men got there, his own mutinous white troops turned on him and fired their muskets. Trumbull was forced to take cover in a nearby house where bullets hit the wooden door and walls.[30]

Trumbull's reinforcements scattered the white rioters and got the survivors of the Fifty-Seventh to safety. Private Edwin J. Munn of the Ninth Iowa wrote:

> ...it took one half the regiment to guard the other till they could get the Negro Regt. away. The boys was so enraged about being sold for a gold watch and then being brigaded with Negros they would not stand it. The next raid they make will be on the officers if things don't change for the better.[31]

The riot leaders took to the hills, but Trumbull sent patrols out after them and most were captured the next day. Trumbull pressed charges against the captured men. It is not known how many blacks were killed or wounded in the riot, but Private Munn wrote, "The Negro loss was 19 killed and a good many wounded."[32]

The army chose to ignore the incident. The charges against the ring-leaders were dropped. The regiment itself, however, ceased to exist as a unit. Trumbull, three "loyal" companies of the Ninth, and the Fifty-Seventh Colored were transferred to Fort Smith, Arkansas. The other companies were sent to different assignments across the state. No mention of the riot and the killings is contained in any published record of the three regiments involved.[33]

In February 1866, the separated companies of the Ninth Iowa Cavalry were ordered to assemble at Little Rock to be mustered out; the soldiers' enlistments were over. Trumbull remained at Fort Smith, and did not bother to attend the ceremony. He sent this message to be read to the men.

> Gentlemen: We are about to separate. Our work is done. The flag of the Republic waves triumphantly over all her domain. In the great struggle which has passed, you have done well, and you leave the service carrying with you a noble tribute of approbation from the Major General commanding the district,...The hardships and dangers you have undergone have been great, and many of our comrades have sunk by the wayside. The discipline has been severe but it was necessary to make

soldiers of you. In the new positions you are to assume, preserve your soldiers' name untainted, and, should the President of the United States again order the long roll beaten, I trust we shall be ready to fall in.

May prosperity and happiness attend you all. Comrades I bid you farewell.
M. M. Trumbull, Colonel
Ninth Iowa Cavalry Volunteers and
Brevet Brigadier General U.S.V. [34]

Epilogue: Wheelbarrow

On 28 February 1866, Matthew Trumbull was mustered out of the army at Little Rock, Arkansas, and made the long trip back to peacetime Iowa. The great summer welcome home celebrations had finished months earlier. No parade greeted Trumbull, nor did he ride at the head of his slickly mounted regiment. He made no speeches to cheering crowds. He was just another former officer in a worn uniform, riding a train home.

Trumbull was reunited with his sons and quietly reopened his Cedar Falls law office. However, he did not remain in Black Hawk County. He tried farming on a small place near Davenport but did not keep at it for long. In the spring of 1866 he met Francis (Fannie) Carroll, a twenty-six-year-old divorcee with a nine-year-old daughter, Florence. Matthew and Fannie had a June wedding and Florence became Florence Trumbull. The couple set up housekeeping in Dubuque and a year later they had a daughter, Alma. With four sons and two daughters, Trumbull was a full-time family man.[1]

At the end of the war, William Stone was governor of Iowa, and the next year John Scott was elected lieutenant governor. Republican former Union officers dominated the next generation of politicians. Trumbull remained an active Republican and was elected district attorney. When Ulysses S. Grant was elected president in 1868, Trumbull claimed his share of the spoils that came with Yankee victory.

> When I came home from the war, I was immediately elected to the office of District Attorney, without any effort of mine, and when General Grant became president, he appointed me Collector of Internal Revenue, also without any solicitation from me. I held that office during the whole of his administration, and although the collection of millions of dollars is a grave responsibility which makes a man tumble and toss about in his bed at night, I met with no disaster and no loss.[2]

In 1877, Trumbull resigned his position and left Iowa. He took his wife and daughter on an extended trip to England, his first visit in thirty years. When he returned from England he brought his brother, Edward, with him. Edward became a farmer in Hardin County, Iowa.[3]

Trumbull sold his Iowa home, moved to Chicago in 1882, and began a new part of his life. He had been an American immigrant, a pioneer lawyer, a politician, and a Union officer. Now he became an author, essayist, and lecturer. His subject, as always, was the fight for the dignity of the working class. His best-known book, *The Free Trade Struggle in England,* came as a result of his journey to England. It was published in 1885, went into at least two editions, and became one of the standard texts on the subject.

Though Trumbull was getting close to sixty, he plunged into the world of Chicago radicalism. No other city quite exemplified the political and labor struggles of the post-Civil War industrial revolution as did Chicago. Carl Sandburg captured the city in poetry while Chicago inspired Upton Sinclair's socialist polemic, *The Jungle.* Chicago was the battleground for the Knights of Labor and other radicals. Union organizers, socialists, and anarchists preached and organized there. Workers in the tens of thousands responded and took to the streets demanding reform. For the aging Trumbull it was a reincarnation of London and his Chartist youth. In fact a few of the other activists were old Chartists who had found a place in American radicalism.

Trumbull became a columnist, and later an editor, for the radical weekly, *The Open Court Press.* He signed his columns "Wheelbarrow," a tribute to the honest labor of his youth. Wheelbarrow always emphasized his belief that real work, work that accomplished something, was morally uplifting, something that liberated a person.

> To work and produce nothing is torture. The divine quality of labor is proved by the pleasure that its product brings. Whether the profit of it comes to the worker or not, it is a satisfaction to know that by his work something exists that did not exist before, or it exists in better shape.[4]

Wheelbarrow went so far as to apply this principle to women and lectured the labor movement on its exclusion of women.

> The equal right of women to work at "skilled labor" is evidence that we are emerging from that social barbarism which consigned one part of them to the bondage of the kitchen, another to the insipid languor of the drawing room, another to a dependence on man's wickedness, so pitiful and so sad that we fear to look upon it lest it show us the reflection of our own guilt, and make our consciences rebel within us at the savagery of man. "Skilled labor" is one of the blessed agencies that shall redeem women from poverty, from wash-tub slavery, and from sin.[5]

Wheelbarrow's major role was that of an aging radical trying to give common sense advice to a new generation that was often more impatient than the old Chartists and abolitionists. He firmly rejected the radical call to violence and revolution. He reminded his readers that in the United States he had found the very thing the Chartists had failed to win in England—access to political power through the vote.

Epilogue: Wheelbarrow

Things were not perfect in America—there was no worker's paradise—but Chartists never demanded paradise. They demanded opportunity, and opportunity came at the ballot box. Trumbull told his radical audience this:

> So long as I have the ballot I am a friend of order; take it away from me and I become a revolutionist....The ballot is the safety valve of American society. So long as I have equality of rights and opportunities I will never complain that my neighbor is rich while I am poor. Take away the ballot from the working man, and instead of a police force you would need an army to preserve your privileges and your property.[6]

On the subject of a worker's revolution, Wheelbarrow wrote:

> Brothers, unless we are ready to open the recruiting offices, let us not talk about fighting. By doing so we expose our own weakness. We bring derision upon ourselves and contempt upon our cause. That is not the worst of it; we undervalue the moral force which we hold in our hands....It is neither wise nor patriotic to persuade the working men that their moral resources are all exhausted, and there is no reform power in the ballot, in the press, and in public opinion. The statement is not true; and the men who make it present us with a dilemma of double despair. Without arms, discipline, leaders, or even a plan of battle, fighting is clearly hopeless. If the ballot is impotent also, then we must fall back for comfort on bombast and beer. We can fill ourselves with the nectar of the gods at five cents a glass, and boast of our intention at some future time to paint the universe red.[7]

Trumbull's most famous fight as a Chicago radical concerned the case of the Haymarket anarchists. On 4 May 1886, Chicago police broke up a large labor rally at the Haymarket Square. A bomb thrown at the police exploded, killing seven police officers and wounding seventy more. The police fired into the crowd and killed four. The terrible incident made national headline news, and conservative editors and politicians used it to emphasize the danger of radicalism in America. The image of the bomb throwing radical was used to taint every reform movement. A month later eight men, all admitted anarchists, were accused of the crime, brought to trial, and convicted. Seven were sentenced to death and one got up to fifteen years in prison. The verdict was appealed but both the Illinois Supreme Court and the U.S. Supreme Court upheld the convictions. The only hope for the convicted anarchists was for Illinois Governor Richard J. Oglesby to grant clemency.

Matthew Trumbull was no anarchist, but he became convinced that the men had not received a fair trial. Labor unions supported the convicted anarchists, as did many reform organizations. Trumbull, along with such literary figures as William Dean Howells and Henry Demerest Lloyd, wrote articles and books in their defense that questioned the trial. Trumbull wrote an article titled "Judge Gary and the Anarchists" and a pamphlet titled *Was It a Fair Trial?* He also donated the $250.00 profit from the pamphlet to the wife of one of the convicted anarchists.[8]

Trumbull visited the men in their cells and visited their families on the outside. He also offered legal advice, though he did not practice law in Illinois. On 8 November 1887, three days before the death sentence was to be carried out, Trumbull was part of a citizen's delegation that traveled to the capital at Springfield to make one last plea to Governor Oglesby. The governor had been a Union officer in the war and when Trumbull spoke it was "as an old soldier who has fought on the battlefield with you . . ."[9]

As a result, the governor commuted the sentences of two of the men to life in prison. However, four others were executed

Matthew Mark Trumbull
"Wheelbarrow"
(*Drawing by Ron Prahl*)

on schedule, and one man hanged himself in his cell rather than be executed by the state.

After the executions Trumbull was one of many radicals and reformers who founded the Amnesty Association, a lobby group dedicated to gaining amnesty for the last, imprisoned Haymarket anarchists. The cause became one of the great rallying points for American radicals. The organization did not succeed under Governor Oglesby or his successor, Joseph Fifer, but with the election of John Peter Altgeld, the Amnesty Association succeeded in gaining pardons for the anarchists. The men were released and returned to Chicago. At the banquet to celebrate the occasion, Matthew Trumbull was honored for the part he played.[10]

Trumbull's radicalism and his "Wheelbarrow" identity never detracted from his pride in having been a Union soldier. He was an active member of Chicago's U.S. Grant Post of the Grand Army of the Republic. There he was called "The Soldier's Friend" because he used his legal skills to help veterans get the bounties and pensions to which they were entitled.[11]

Trumbull's war wounds, his bronchitis, and kidney disease finally took their toll. He was ill throughout the winter of 1893-94, and on 9 May 1894, he died at sixty-eight years old. He was buried in a Chicago cemetery, attended by his wife, daughter, at least one of his sons, and many friends. If Trumbull had written his own epitaph, it would not be much different than these words from one of his Wheelbarrow columns.

Epilogue: Wheelbarrow

It sounds conceited to hear a poor man boast of having lived a life of luxury, and yet I make that boast. I make it, I trust with becoming modesty, but after all with pride.…To be sure, I was born rich. I came into this world with a large capital in the shape of health and vitality to my credit in the bank,…I have worked from dawn till dark at the hardest kind of labor, with pick and shovel and wheelbarrow …but I was proud of the health and strength that enabled me to do it: and the consciousness that I was a free citizen whose vote was equal in power to that of a millionaire, made life not only worth living, but a revelry of enjoyment. When the high-cast party challenged the low-caste party to fight it out, I stood by my order, the low-caste party, and fought it out on that line, not only all summer, but for four summers, and four winters too. When the bullets knocked me over, as they sometimes did, I let the doctors patch me up again, and came forward for another round. At the end of the dispute it was my supreme luxury to "stand up stiddy in the ranks," as the low-caste banner went up and the high-caste banner went down, and I saw the flag of slavery furled forever.[12]

Notes

Foreword

1. Wheelbarrow (Matthew Mark Trumbull), *Articles and Discussions on the Labor Question* (Chicago: The Open Court Publishing Company, 1890), 151 (hereafter cited as Wheelbarrow).

Chapter 1: The Chartist

1. Wheelbarrow, 11.
2. Ibid.
3. Ibid., 12.
4. Ibid., 14.
5. Ibid., 14-15.
6. Ibid., 16.
7. Ibid., 66.
8. Ibid., 18-91.
9. George Rude, *The Crowd in History, 1730-1848* (New York: John Wiley & Sons, Inc., 1964), 181.
10. Ibid.
11. Wheelbarrow, 20.

Chapter 2: My Light is None the Less for Lighting My Neighbor

1. Wheelbarrow, 21.
2. Ibid., 22.
3. Ibid., 22.
4. Ibid., 26.
5. Ibid., 28.
6. Ibid., 50-51.
7. Ibid., 29.
8. Ibid., 30.
9. U.S. Census Office, Eighth Census, 1860 (Washington, D.C.: National Archives and Records Service, 1967), Buchanan To Chickasaw Counties, Iowa (hereafter cited as 1860 Census).
10. Wheelbarrow, 32.

11. Ibid., 32.

12. Ibid., 33.

13. 1860 Census.

14. Wheelbarrow, 56.

15. Virginius Dabney, *Richmond: The Story of a City* (New York: Doubleday and Company, Inc., 1976), 139.

16. Wheelbarrow, 34.

Chapter 3: Iowa

1. Wheelbarrow, 35.

2. Ibid.

3. Ibid., 36.

4. Rudolf Priepke, *Years Ago: A Commemorative Edition in Honor of Clarksville's Quasquicentennial,* (Clarksville, Iowa: The Star Corp., 1978), 12.

5. *History of Butler and Bremer Counties, Iowa,* (Springfield, Illinois: Union Publishing Company, 1883), 240-241.

6. Ibid., 330-331.

7. 1860 Census.

8. Benjamin F. Gue, *History of Iowa,* 4 vols., (New York City, The Century History Company, 1903), 1:353.

9. Wheelbarrow, 36.

10. Dan Elbert Clark, *Samuel Jordan Kirkwood,* (Iowa City, Iowa: The State Historical Society of Iowa, 1917), 76

11. Gue, 4:30.

12. Ibid., 111.

13. Ibid., 80.

14. Ibid., 17.

15. Peter Melendy, "Zimri Streeter—'Old Black Hawk,'" *Annals of Iowa,* 3rd Series, 1 (August 1894): 414.

16. Gue, 4:180.

17. Benjamin F. Shambaugh, ed. *Documentary Material Relating to the History of Iowa* 6 vols. (Iowa City, Iowa: The State Historical Society of Iowa, 1897), 1:226.

18. Leland L. Sage, *A History of Iowa* (Iowa State University Press, 1974), 61, 140.

19. Gue, 1:357.

20. Shambaugh, 1:226.

21. Wheelbarrow, 36-37.

22. Melendy, 14. Bess Streeter Aldrich, *Song of Years* (New York: Grosset & Dunlap Publishers, 1939), 226.

23. Wheelbarrow, 38.

Chapter 4: The Butler County Union Guards

1. Wheelbarrow, 37.
2. *Roster and Record of Iowa Soldiers in the War of the Rebellion* 6 Vols. (Des Moines: Iowa General Assembly, 1908-1911), 1:3 (hereafter cited as *Roster and Record*).
3. Clark, 180-181.
4. *Roster and Record*, 1:4.
5. *Butler County Jeffersonian*, 4 May 1861.
6. Ibid., 18 May 1861.
7. Ibid.
8. *Cedar Falls Gazette*, 13 September 1861.
9. Ray Boston, "General Matthew Mark Trumbull: Respectable Radical," *Journal of the Illinois Historical Society*, 66 (Summer 1973): 168.
10. *Cedar Falls Gazette*, 31 May 1861.
11. *Dubuque Daily Times*, 21 April 1861.
12. Wheelbarrow, 38-39.
13. *Roster and Record*, 1:4.
14. Luella M. Wright, "The Pioneer Greys," *Palimpsest* 22 (January, 1941): 30.
15. Priepke, 12. 1870 Census. (National Archives and Records).
16. *Cedar Falls Gazette*, 7 June 1861.
17. Ibid.
18. *Waterloo Courier*, 5 June 1861.
19. Ibid.
20. *Dubuque Daily Times*, 5 June 1861.
21. *Cedar Falls Gazette*, 7 June 1861.
22. Ibid.
23. Ibid.
24. Lieutenant S. D. Thompson, *Recollections With the Third Iowa Regiment* (Cincinnati: By the author, 1864), 19.
25. *Butler County Jeffersonian*, 20 June 1861.

Chapter 5: The Matter of Rank

1. Clark, 213.
2. Gue, 4:129-130.
3. Thompson, 20.
4. Ibid., 19.
5. Gue, 4:288.
6. Henry L. Stout, "Letter To Governor Kirkwood," 28 May 1861. *Records of Colo-*

nel Nelson G. Williams, Adjutant General of Iowa, General Correspondence, Civil War, 1861. State Historical Society of Iowa, Des Moines.

7. Leland L. Sage, *William Boyd Allison: A Study In Practical Politics* (Iowa City: State Historical Society of Iowa, 1956), 30.

8. William Boyd Allison. "Letter To Governor Kirkwood," 27 May 1861. *Records of Colonel Nelson G. Williams, Adjutant General of Iowa, General Correspondence, Civil War, 1861.* State Historical Society of Iowa, Des Moines.

9. "Minutes Of Officers' Meeting," 17 June 1861. *Records of the Third Iowa Infantry, Adjutant General of Iowa, General Correspondence, Civil War, 1861.* State Historical Society of Iowa, Des Moines.

10. Gue, 4:253.

11 "Minutes of Officers' Meeting," 17 June 1861.

12. Ibid.

13. Gue, 4:235.

14. John Scott, "Letter To Governor Kirkwood," 25 July 1861. *Records of Colonel Nelson G. Williams, Adjutant General of Iowa, General Correspondence, Civil War, 1861.* State Historical Society of Iowa, Des Moines.

15. Thompson, 27, 31.

16. Ibid., 40.

17. Ibid., 40-41.

Chapter 6: The Shelbina Affair

1. Thompson, 67.

2. *Butler County Jeffersonian,* 26 August 1861.

3. Thompson, 41.

4. *Butler County Jeffersonian,* 27 July 1861.

5. Ibid.

6. Thompson, 48.

7. *Butler County Jeffersonian,* 27 July 1861.

8. Thompson, 59.

9. *Butler County Jeffersonian,* 27 July 1861.

10. Ibid.

11. "Petition From Officers of The Third Iowa Infantry, To General S. A. Hurlbut," 12 August 1861. *Records of Colonel Nelson G. Williams, Adjutant General of Iowa, General Correspondence, Civil War, 1861.* State Historical Society of Iowa, Des Moines.

12. Larry J. Daniel, *Shiloh: The Battle That Changed The Civil War* (New York: Simon and Schuster, 1997), 188.

13. Thomas O. Edwards, "Letter To Governor Kirkwood," 24 August 1861. *Records*

of Colonel Nelson G. Williams, Adjutant General of Iowa, General Correspondence, Civil War, 1861. State Historical Society of Iowa, Des Moines.

14. Thompson, 107.

15. Ibid., 109.

16. Ibid.

17. General John Pope, "Charges and Specifications Against Colonel N. B. Williams, 3rd Iowa Regiment," September 1861. *Records Of Colonel Nelson G. Williams, Adjutant General Of Iowa, General Correspondence, Civil War, 1861.* State Historical Society of Iowa, Des Moines.

18. Thompson, 106.

19. *Cedar Falls Gazette,* 20 September 1861.

Chapter 7: The Battle of Blue Mills Landing

1. *Dubuque Weekly Times,* 17 October 1861.

2. Ibid.

3. Ibid.

4. Ibid.

5. Charles P. Brown, "The Battle of Blue Mills Landing," *Annals of Iowa,* 3ʳᵈ Series, 14 (April 1924): 290.

6. Ibid.

7. *Dubuque Weekly Times,* 17 October 1861.

8. Ibid.

9. Brown, 291.

10. Ibid.

11. *Roster and Record,* 1:294-399.

12. "Report of Lt. Col. John Scott," United States War Department, *The War of the Rebellion: A Compilation of the Official Records of the Union and Confederate Armies,* 70 vols. in 128 (Washington, DC, 1880-1901), Series 1, 1:93-194 (hereafter cited as *Official Records*).

13. *Dubuque Weekly Times,* 17 October 1861.

Chapter 8: The Battle of Pittsburg Landing (Shiloh)

1. *Dubuque Weekly Times,* 17 October 1861.

2. Thompson, 88, 167.

3. Ibid., 169-170.

4. Ibid., 171.

5. "Letter to Asst. Adj. Gen.," 24 October 1861. *Military Records of Col. Nelson G. Williams,* National Archives and Records.

6. "Letter From Governor Kirkwood to General J. C. Frémont," 1 September 1861. *Military Records of Col. Nelson G. Williams,* National Archives and Records.

7. "Letter from John Scott to General Halleck," 27 November 1861. *Military Records of Col. Nelson G. Williams,* National Archives.

8. "Letter From Col. Nelson G. Williams to General Halleck," 20 December 1861. *Military Records of Col. Nelson G. Williams,* National Archives.

9. "Special Order From General Halleck," 5 December 1861. *Military Records of Col. Nelson G. Williams,* National Archives.

10. "Letter From Col. Nelson G. Williams To General Halleck," 6 December 1861. *Military Records of Col. Nelson G. Williams, Adjutant General of Iowa, General Correspondence, Civil War, 1861.* State Historical Society of Iowa, Des Moines.

11. Thompson, 188.

12. *Dubuque Daily Times,* 1 March 1862.

13. Thompson, 188.

14. *Cedar Falls Gazette,* 22 November 1861.

15. Thompson, 188.

16. *Roster and Record*, 1:337.

17. Captain A. A. Stuart, *Iowa Colonels and Regiments: Being a History of Iowa Regiments in the War of the Rebellion* (Des Moines: Mills and Co., 1865), 93.

18. Ulysses S. Grant, *Memoirs and Selected Letters 1839-1865* (The Library of America, 1990), 223.

19. Thompson, 206-207.

20. John Hilary Kellenbarger, "The War Years," Unpublished manuscript, Kellenbarger File, State Historical Society of Iowa, Des Moines, 15.

21. Thompson, 213.

22. Ibid.

23. Ibid., 215.

24. Ibid.

25. Kellenbarger, 16-17.

26. Ibid., 18.

27. George W. Crosley, "Some Reminiscences of an Iowa Soldier," *Annals of Iowa,* 3rd Series 10 (July 1911): 130.

28. Daniel, 236.

29. Mark Mayo Boatner III, *The Civil War Dictionary* (New York: David McKay Company, Inc., 1959), 757.

30. *Roster and Record*, 1:294-398.

31. "Report of Captain Matthew M. Trumbull," 17 April 1862. *Official Records,* Series 1, 3:219.

Chapter 9: The Hero of the Hatchie

1. *Cedar Falls Gazette,* 16 May 1862.
2. Ibid., 25 April 1862.
3. Thompson, 249.
4. *Dubuque Daily Times,* 29 April 1862.
5. Stuart, 476. *Cedar Falls Gazette,* 19 September 1862.
6. *Roster and Record,* 1:294.
7. *Dubuque Daily Times,* 15 July 1862.
8. Ibid.
9. Ibid., 11 September 1862.
10. Stuart, 9-10.
11. *Dubuque Daily Times,* 30 April 1862.
12. Ibid.
13. "Letter To Governor Kirkwood From the Officers of The Third Iowa Infantry," 29 June 1862. *Records of the Third Iowa Infantry, Adjutant General of Iowa, General Correspondence, Civil War, 1862.* State Historical Society of Iowa, Des Moines.
14. Thompson, 281.
15. "Letter to Colonel Nelson G. Williams," 17 July 1862. *Military Records of Matthew M. Trumbull,* National Archives.
16. Thompson, 291.
17. Ibid., 298.
18. Ibid., 288.
19. Wheelbarrow, 90-91.
20. Boston, 168.
21. Wheelbarrow, 272.
22. *Dubuque Daily Times,* 17 October 1862.
23. *Cedar Falls Gazette,* 17 October 1862.
24. Ibid.
25. Thompson, 312.
26. *Roster and Record,* 294-399.
27. Thompson, 315.
28. "Report of Lt. Col. Matthew M. Trumbull," 8 October 1862. *Official Records,* Series 1, 17, Pt. 1:316.

Chapter 10: Tattoo

1. Thompson, 321.
2. Ibid.
3. "Letter From Lt. Col. Matthew M. Trumbull To Adjutant, Third Iowa Infantry,"

17 November 1862. *Military Records of Matthew M. Trumbull*, National Archives and Records.

4. Ibid.

5. Thompson, 341.

6. *Butler County Stars and Stripes*, 10 December 1862.

7. Ibid.

8. Thompson, 342.

9. Ibid.

10. "Letter From Col. Nelson G. Williams To Adjutant, Third Iowa Infantry," 28 November 1862. *Military Records of Col. Nelson G. Williams*, National Archives and Records.

11. Stuart, 96.

12. "Letter To Governor Kirkwood From the Officers of the Third Iowa Infantry," 4 December 1862. *Records of The Third Iowa Infantry, Adjutant General of Iowa, Civil War, 1862*. State Historical Society of Iowa, Des Moines.

13. *Dubuque Daily Times*, 19 December 1862.

Chapter 11: The Ninth Iowa Cavalry

1. Wheelbarrow, 68.

2. *Cedar Falls Gazette*, 12 December 1862.

3. *Cedar Falls Gazette*, 13 March 1863, 20 May 1863.

4. *Dubuque Daily Times*, 18 February 1863.

5. "Letter to Governor Kirkwood From Assistant Adjutant General," 20 December 1862, *Adjutant General of Iowa, General Correspondence, Civil War, 1862*. State Historical Society, Des Moines.

6. Cassius C. Stiles, "The Skunk River War (Or Tally War)," *Annals of Iowa*, 3rd Series, 19 (April 1935): 622.

7. Ibid., 629.

8. *Roster and Record*, 1:294-399.

9. *Dubuque Daily Times*, 13 September 1863.

10. Sage, 164.

11. *Roster and Record*, 4:1656-1767.

12. Ibid., 1656.

13. Ibid., 2:469. *Dubuque Daily Times*, 4 November 1863.

14. *Roster and Record*, 4:1657.

15. "Letter To Governor Kirkwood From M. M. Trumbull," 16 November 1863. *Records of the Ninth Iowa Cavalry, Adjutant General of Iowa, General Correspondence, Civil War*. State Historical Society of Iowa. Des Moines.

16. *Roster and Record*, 4:1656.

17. Quoted in the *Dubuque Daily Times,* 11 December 1863.

18. *Dubuque Daily Times,* 22 December 1863.

19. *Roster and Record*, 1:308, 331.

20. Ibid., 5:1585-1587.

21. *Dubuque Daily Times,* 22 December 1863.

22. *Roster and Record*, 4:1040.

23. *The Encyclopedia of the American Civil War,* 5 vols., (Santa Barbara, CA: ABC CLIO, 2000), 1:72.

24. "Letter From Sergeant Edwin J. Munn, Ninth Iowa Cavalry," 27 March 1865. Private Collection of Mr. Eugene P. Jorgensen, Lincoln, Nebraska. (Copies of the original letter in the collection of Kenneth L. Lyftogt, University of Northern Iowa.)

25. *Roster and Record*, 5:1652.

26. "Report of the Assistant Inspector General," 21 January 1865. *Official Records,* Ser. 1, 48, Pt. 1:600.

27. Frederick H. Dyer, *A Compendium of the War of the Rebellion,* 3 vols., (New York: Thomas Yoseloff, 1959), 3:1733.

28. Ed Bearss and Arrell M. Gibson, *Fort Smith, Little Gibraltar on the Arkansas* (Norman: University of Oklahoma Press, 1969), 3008.

29. *Roster and Record*, 4:1653.

30. "Letter of Sergeant Edwin J. Munn, Ninth Iowa Cavalry," 12 July 1865. (Private collection of Mr. Eugene P. Jorgensen).

31. Ibid.

32. Ibid.

33. *Roster and Record*, 4:1654. See also Military Records of Daniel L. Ochiltree, William C. Wilson, and Charles E. Osterhaut, Ninth Iowa Cavalry, National Archive and Records.

34. *Roster and Record*, 4:1654-1655.

Epilogue: Wheelbarrow

1. *Pension Records of Matthew M. Trumbull,* Nation Archives. U.S. Census Records, 1870, Dubuque. Iowa.

2. Wheelbarrow, 40.

3. Boston, 169.

4. Wheelbarrow, 96.

5. Ibid., 79.

6. Ibid., 88.

7. Ibid., 72-73.

8. Boston, 172.

9. Ibid., 171.

10. Ibid., 174.
11. Brigham Johnson, *Iowa: Its History and Its Foremost Citizens* (Chicago: J. J. Clarke Publishing Co., 1915), 385-386.
12. Wheelbarrow, 82.

Bibliography

Adjutant General's Records. Records of the Ninth Iowa Cavalry. General Correspondence, Civil War. State Historical Society of Iowa, Des Moines, Iowa.

Adjutant General's Records. Records of the Third Iowa Volunteer Infantry. General Correspondence, Civil War. State Historical Society of Iowa, Des Moines, Iowa.

Bearss, Ed and Arrell M. Gibson. *Fort Smith, Little Gibraltar on the Arkansas.* Norman, OK: University of Oklahoma Press, 1969.

Bergman, Leola N. "The Negro in Iowa." *Iowa Journal of History and Politics* 44 (January 1948): 3-89.

Boston, Ray. "General Matthew Mark Trumbull: Respectable Radical." *Journal of the Illinois Historical Society* 66 (Summer 1973): 159-76.

Brown, Charles P. "The Battle of Blue Mills Landing." *Annals of Iowa* 3rd Series, 14 (April 1924): 287-94.

Butler County Stars and Stripes, 1862.

The Butler County Jeffersonian, 1861-1862.

Byers, S. H. M. *Iowa in Wartime.* Des Moines, IA: W. W. Condit and Co., 1888.

Cedar Falls Gazette, 1861-1865.

Clark, Dan Elbert. *Samuel Jordon Kirkwood.* Iowa City, IA: State Historical Society of Iowa, 1917.

Colbert, Thomas B. "Remembering Francis Jay Herron, Iowa's Forgotten Hero." Unpublished manuscript. Marshalltown Community College, Marshalltown, IA.

Crosley, George W. "Some Reminiscences of an Iowa Soldier." *Annals of Iowa,* 3rd Series, 10 (July 1910): 119-136.

Bibliography

Dabney, Virginius. *Richmond: The Story of a City.* New York: Doubleday and Company, Inc., 1976.

Daniel, Larry J. Shiloh: *The Battle That Changed The Civil War.* New York: Simon & Schuster, 1997.

Dubuque Daily Times, 1861-1865.

Dubuque Weekly Times, 1861–1863.

Dyer, Frederick H. *A Compendium of the War of the Rebellion.* 3 vols. New York: Thomas Yoseoff, 1959.

The Encyclopedia of the American Civil War. 5 vols. Santa Barbara, CA: ABC CLIO, 2000.

Foote, Shelby. *The Civil War.* 3 vols. New York: Random House, 1958.

Glatthaar, Joseph T. Forged in Battle: *The Civil War Alliance of Black Soldiers and White Officers.* New York: The Free Press, 1990.

Grant, Ulysses S. *Memoirs and Selected Letters.* New York: The Library of America, 1990.

Gue, Benjamin F. *History of Iowa.* 4 vols. New York: Century History Co., 1903.

History of Butler and Bremer Counties, Iowa. Springfield, IL: Union Publishing Co., 1883.

Ingersoll, Lurton D. *Iowa and the Rebellion.* Philadelphia: J. B. Lippincott and Co., 1866.

Johnson, Brigham. *Iowa: Its History and Its Foremost Citizens.* 3 vols. Chicago: S. J. Clark Publishing Co., 1915.

Kellenbarger, John Hilary, Third Iowa Infantry and Ninth Iowa Cavalry. "The War Years" and other letters. Kellenbarger File, State Historical Society of Iowa, Des Moines, IA.

Keokuk Gate City, 1861.

Lathrop, H. W. *The Life and Times of Samuel J. Kirkwood: Iowa's War Governor.* Iowa City: State Historical Society of Iowa and the Author, 1893.

Learner, Max. *America as a Civilization.* New York: Simon and Schuster, 1957.

McClain, Emlin. "Charles Mason—Iowa's First Jurist." *Annals of Iowa,* 3rd Series, 4 (January 1901): 597-600.

Melendy, Peter. "Zimri Streeter—'Old Black Hawk'." *Annals of Iowa,* 3rd Series, 1 (August 1894): 412-15.

Letters of Sergeant Edwin J. Munn, Ninth Iowa Cavalry. Private Collection of Mr. Eugene P. Jorgensen, Lincoln, NE.

Ochiltree, Daniel L., Ninth Iowa Cavalry. *Military Records.* National Archives and Records Administration.

Osterhaut, Charles E., Ninth Iowa Cavalry. *Military Records.* National Archives and Records Administration.

Priepke, Rudolf. *Years Ago: A Commemorative Edition in Honor of Clarksville's Quasquicentennial.* Clarksville, IA: The Starr Corp., 1978.

Rosenberg, Morton M. *Iowa on the Eve of the Civil War.* Norman: University of Oklahoma Press, 1972.

Rosenblatt, Frank F. *The Chartist Movement.* New York: Columbia University, P.S. King & Son, LTD, 1916.

Roster and Record of Iowa Soldiers in the War of the Rebellion. 6 vols. Des Moines, IA: Iowa General Assembly, 1908-1911.

Rude, George. *The Crowd in History, 1730-1848.* New York: John Wiley & Sons, Inc., 1964.

Sage, Leland L. *A History of Iowa.* Ames: Iowa State University Press, 1974.

_____. *William Boyd Allison: A Study in Practical Politics.* Iowa City, IA: State Historical Society of Iowa, 1956.

Bibliography

Shaara, Michael. *The Killer Angels*. New York: Random House, 1974.

Shambaugh, Benjamin F. *Documentary Material Relating to the History of Iowa*. 6 vols. Iowa City: State Historical Society of Iowa, 1897.

Stiles, Cassius C. "The Skunk River War (Or Tally War)." *Annals of Iowa*, 3rd Series, 19 (April 1935): 614-631.

Stuart, Captain A. A., *Iowa Colonels and Regiments: Being a History of Iowa Regiments of the War of the Rebellion*. Des Moines, IA: Mills and Co., 1865.

Thompson, Lieutenant S. D. *Recollections With the Third Iowa Regiment*. Cincinnati: By the Author, 1864.

Trumbull, Matthew Mark. *Military and Pension Records*. National Archives and Records Administration.

U.S. Department of Commerce, Bureau of Census, Eighth Census, 1860. National Archives and Records Service, 1967. Roll 313, Buchanan to Chickasaw Counties, IA.

Waterloo Courier, 1861-1866.

Wheelbarrow (Matthew Mark Trumbull). *Articles and Discussion on the Labor Question*. Chicago: The Open Court Publishing Co., 1890.

Williams, Colonel Nelson G. *Military Records*. National Archives and Records Administration.

Wilson, William C., Ninth Iowa Cavalry. *Military Records*. National Archives and Records Administration.

Wright, Luella M. "The Pioneer Greys." *Palimpsest*, 22 (January 1941): 1-32.

Index

Index